To our five children,
Mark, Megan, Sarah, Paige, and Allie.
We love you. You have taught us an
immeasurable amount about the
magnificence of Jesus. We pray this
book blesses your children and your
children's children in their walk
with the Lamb of God.

The Magnificent Names of Jesus

Good Shepherd
Master
The Truth
True Vine
Lord
The Light
Savior of the World
Son of Man
Great I AM
Lamb of God
The Truth
Cornerstone
Son of Mary and Joseph
Living Water
God's Chosen

Copyright © 2022 by Jimmy and Sally Dodd
Published by B&H Publishing Group, Nashville, Tennessee
Illustrations Copyright © 2022 by B&H Publishing Group
All rights reserved.
ISBN: 978-1-0877-4053-9

Unless otherwise noted, all Scripture quotations are taken from the The Holy Bible, English Standard Version Copyright © 2001 by Crossway Bibles, a publishing ministry of Good News Publishers. Scriptures marked NIV are taken from the Holy Bible, New International Version®, NIV® Copyright ©1973, 1978, 1984, 2011 by Biblica, Inc. Used by permission.
All rights reserved worldwide.
DEWEY: C232
SUBHD: NAMES / JESUS CHRIST--NAME / PERSONAL NAMES
Printed in Colombia, South America in October 2021
1 2 3 4 5 • 25 24 23 22 21

The Magnificent Names of Jesus

Prayers and Praises to Love Him More

Jimmy and Sally Dodd

Illustrated by Paran Kim

And then they will see the Son of Man coming in clouds with great power and glory.
—Mark 13:26

The Magnificent Names of Jesus

Introduction: Why Are Names Important, and Why Does Jesus Have So Many?... 9
1. Jesus Is a Man 12
2. Jesus Is the Son of Man 16
3. Jesus Is the Son of Mary and Joseph 20
4. Jesus Is God's Son 24
5. Jesus Is a Teacher 28
6. Jesus Is God 32
7. Jesus Is Lord 36
8. Jesus Is the Christ 40
9. Jesus Is King 44
10. Jesus Is the Holy One 48
11. Jesus Is a Friend 52
12. Jesus Is the Great I AM 56
13. Jesus Is God's Chosen 60
14. Jesus Is the Light 64
15. Jesus Is the Bread of Life 68
16. Jesus Is Living Water 72

17 Jesus Is the Prophet	76
18 Jesus Is the Horn of Salvation	80
19 Jesus Is the One Who Came Down from Heaven	84
20 Jesus Is the Great Physician	88
21 Jesus Is Master	92
22 Jesus Is the Good Shepherd	96
23 Jesus Is a Carpenter	100
24 Jesus Is the Truth	104
25 Jesus Is the Bridegroom	108
26 Jesus Is the True Vine	112
27 Jesus of Nazareth	116
28 Jesus Is the Hope of Israel	120
29 Jesus Is the Savior of the World	124
30 Jesus Is the Cornerstone	128
31 Jesus Is the Door	132
32 Jesus Is the Stairway to Heaven	136
33 Jesus Is the One	140
34 Jesus Is Called Sir (the One to Whom Respect Is Due)	144
35 Jesus Is a Big Brother	148
36 Jesus Is the Lamb of God	152
37 The Names in John's Revelation	156
Jesus Knows Your Name	160

Why Are Names Important, and Why Does Jesus Have So Many?

Think about your name. You have a first name and a last name. You might also have a middle name. Do you know what your name means or why your parents gave you that name? Maybe you have a nickname. It could be a funny name or a name that really describes you.

Names are important! When you hear people say your name, you look at them and wonder what they want to say to you.

And if you meet somebody who has your same name, you probably get excited and can't wait to tell them that you have the same name!

Can you imagine if all our names were alike? What if we were all in the same classroom with the same name? How would we know who the teacher was talking to? How would we know whose turn it was to be the line leader or a special helper?

Our names tell the world who we are and what we are to be called. Our names are special because they were given to us!

Jesus has many magnificent names that tell us many wonderful things about Him too. His names tell us so much about who He is!

In this book, we are going to discover the names of Jesus used in the Gospels, the stories of Jesus written by four men—Matthew, Mark, Luke, and John. Do you know that in just these four Gospels, Jesus has more than one hundred different names? That's a lot of names. In just the first chapter of John, some of Jesus' names are: *The Word, God, Light of All Mankind, True Light, Only Begotten of the Father, One Greater than John the Baptist, Jesus Christ, Lord, the Lamb of God, the One Who Baptizes with the Holy Spirit, God's Chosen One, Son of God, Rabbi, Messiah, the One About Whom Moses and the Prophets Wrote, King of Israel, Stairway Between God and Mankind.*

All those names can be found in just one chapter! Did you know Jesus was called so many different names? Jesus is so powerful, so loving, and so amazing that there could probably never be enough names to describe Him.

We can talk to Jesus and call Him by His different names. They all belong to Him, kind of like nicknames, but these names have very special meanings. The more we know about the names of Jesus, the more we know about our Savior!

We can also use any of these beautiful and special names to pray to Jesus, because they all belong to Him.

Special note: We talk about mommies and daddies in this book. But we know all families are different. Some of you may live with just your mommy or just your daddy. Some of you live with a foster mommy and daddy. Some of you live with your grandparents. We hope all of you live with someone who loves and cares for you. When you come to a sentence that talks about mommies and daddies, we encourage those who are reading this book to you to change the words to fit your own unique family. Every family is special to God, including yours!

The person reading you this book loves you, and this book will talk about someone who loves you even more—Jesus. We pray this book will help you learn how to pray to Jesus by using His special names.

Now let's look at some of the magnificent names of Jesus!

Jimmy and Sally Dodd

Dear Jesus,

Thank You for my name. Thank You for a mommy and daddy who gave me my special name.

Thank You for this special book. I pray that as I learn about Your names, I will be reminded to think about their importance for the rest of my life. Help me to learn to pray using Your names.

I pray in the name of my Lord and my Savior Jesus Christ, Amen.

1
Jesus Is a Man

You are a boy or a girl, but do you know what else you are? Human! You have a human body that gets hurt and tired, and each day you experience so many feelings. You might be really happy and then sad. Strong and then tired. Lonely and then angry. That's all a part of being a human person.

Jesus was a person too—a man! But there has never been nor will there ever be another man like Jesus. He lived on the earth like we do and was tempted to do bad things like we are. But unlike us, He lived a perfect life and did not sin. Jesus was the most real man who has ever lived.

Many things in the Bible are a mystery. Some parts can be hard to understand, and it might be difficult to see how it all fits together. One of the great mysteries of the Bible is this: Jesus is both fully man and fully God, at the exact same time!

Jesus wasn't half man and half God. Jesus wasn't two people living in one body. Jesus wasn't God pretending to be a man. He was 100 percent God and 100 percent man. Jesus was completely man and completely God. The human and the holy were joined together in Jesus. That is a wonderful, glorious, important mystery.

Because Jesus was a real man, He had many of the same feelings you and I have every day. Jesus knew what it felt like to be happy and sad. The Bible tells us that at times He was hungry and thirsty. He worked hard and grew tired. He slept. Some days Jesus was so sad that He cried. Other times He was mad, although He never sinned when He was angry. Even though people worshipped Him, Jesus was always willing to serve. He was a humble man.

Because Jesus was a man, He understands how it feels when someone says something that hurts your feelings. He knows what loneliness feels like. After all, on Jesus' most difficult day, His friends ran away, just when He needed them most.

As a man, Jesus knows some things are really hard to do. He understands when you ask your parents if you can skip a chore that you know will be really hard. He's not surprised when you don't want to share. He understands when you are tempted to say something mean.

But don't forget . . . Jesus is also God! He lived a sinless life. He healed people from sickness and brought dead people back to life. Jesus forgave sin. Only God can do that!

Jesus lived among the people and taught them all about God's love. He talked about sin and their need to be forgiven. He showed people how to show that love to others and washed the disciples' dirty, smelly feet as an example. That may sound yucky to us, but Jesus did it to show how He wants us to serve each other, even when it may feel icky or strange or uncomfortable.

Jesus is a man. He is the only man who has ever gone to the cross to pay the price for everyone's sins. But Jesus is not like any other man who has ever lived or who will ever live, because although Jesus is a man, He is also God! If you love and follow Jesus, you have been saved! Jesus being human is just as important to your salvation as Jesus being God. Jesus being God means He is *divine*, which is a wonderful word to help you understand our wonderful Jesus.

Dear Jesus, the Man,

You are fully God and fully man! Thank You for coming from heaven to earth to live as a man and totally experience life. The only way You could save the world was to be a totally perfect, divine person but also be a wholly complete human. And You did just that, for me.

Because You are both human and divine, You can help me when I am tempted. Please help me to look to You for help when I feel like doing things that I know are wrong. The only way You could be God and yet die on a cross is through humility and obedience. Help me to live a humble and obedient life too. Take away the pride that lives within my heart. Give me an obedient heart that is more like Yours.

I pray in the name of Jesus, the only One who was all God and all man.
Amen.

> And the Word became flesh and dwelt among us, and we have seen his glory, glory as of the only Son from the Father, full of grace and truth.
> —John 1:14

Jesus is called…

The Man—John 19:5

Son of Man—John 8:28

That Righteous Man—Matthew 27:19

The Man Who Told You the Truth He Heard from God—John 8:40

Jesus Is the Son of Man

Have you ever played the game where your family hides a toy in your room and you try to find it? When you are far away, they say, "Cold." When you are getting closer, they say, "Warmer," and when you are very close, they say, "Hotter." And when you are just about to find the hidden toy, they say, "Burning!" When your family gives hints or clues, they are helping you arrive at the right destination. Their hints help you find the toy.

When we try to clearly understand who Jesus is, sometimes He gives hints. And if you think deep and hard about the hints He is giving, you will discover more of Jesus' awesome power and amazing love.

Of all the names of Jesus in the four Gospels, He is called *Lord* most of all. But the name He is called the second most might surprise you—the *Son of Man*. He is called *that* more than seventy times in the Gospels.

What is even more important is *Son of Man* is the name Jesus uses the most when referring to Himself. This name gives us a very important hint into understanding who Jesus is and why He has such a deep and wonderful love for you.

To understand the hint Jesus gave by calling Himself *the Son of Man*, we'll go back to the Old Testament, to the book of Daniel. In chapter 7, Daniel tells of a vision where the "Son of Man" comes in the clouds of heaven and stands before God the Father who then gives the Son of Man the power to judge and rule over all the earth. The Son of Man is Lord over every person, every nation, and every language in a kingdom that will never ever end. In Daniel's vision, the Son of Man is a heavenly ruler who is to be lifted up and worshipped.

When Jesus says He is the Son of Man, He is telling us He is the heavenly figure Daniel saw in his vision! Jesus is the Son of Man who is coming in the clouds in power and glory, the forever King whose reign will never end.

In the New Testament, when Jesus was on trial, the most important religious leader asked Him if He was the Christ. Jesus answered yes, and then He said something very important . . . that one day the Son of Man would come on the clouds in glory and power to judge the earth.

Jesus was using the same words Daniel had used when telling people about his vision long ago. Well, the religious leader screamed and told everyone that Jesus had just said He was God. And he was exactly right!

When Jesus calls Himself the Son of Man, He is saying He is God. He is the One who is seated on the clouds wearing a golden crown. He is the One who rules over every person who ever lived, every word that has ever been spoken, and every nation on the whole earth. And the Son of Man loves you!

Think about that. The most powerful person who sits on a throne in the clouds, the One who wears the most beautiful golden crown, the One who rules over everything, and the One who will one day return with His angels—the Son of Man loves you!

Dear Jesus, the Son of Man,

Thank You for giving me important hints so I can know for certain that You are the Son of Man. You are in control of all things. One day You will return to this earth with Your angels to take me home to live with You in Your forever kingdom.

Please help me believe deep in my heart that You are the One who is to be worshipped.

I pray in the name of Jesus, the Son of Man.

Amen.

> And then they will see the Son of Man coming in clouds with great power and glory.
> —Mark 13:26

Jesus is called...

The Son of Man—Matthew 12:8, Mark 2:10, Luke 22:69, John 13:31

Jesus Is the Son of Mary and Joseph

Birthdays are the best! Maybe on your last birthday, your mommy and daddy had a party for you. Maybe your grandma and grandpa were there or you invited some special friends to help you celebrate your big day. Did you have cake and ice cream? Did your friends sing "Happy Birthday" to you? Birthdays are definitely special days.

Another very special day happens on December 25. That's right; it's Christmas . . . the day we celebrate Jesus' birthday! This day is so special that you don't even have to go to school and your family might spend weeks getting ready to celebrate this most important birthday. You spend time together enjoying traditions. Families put up special decorations, buy gifts for the people they love, sing beautiful Christmas carols, and read special books—all to remember and celebrate that Jesus was born.

When you think about Jesus' birthday, you can think about the ways His birth was different from yours. You were probably born in a clean hospital surrounded by doctors and nurses. Jesus wasn't born in a hospital or even a nice, clean house. But still, Jesus was born in a most beautiful way. He was born in the tiny village of Bethlehem, in a room where animals lived. It probably smelled a lot like a barn! No doctors or nurses were nearby to help, but Jesus was born there to His mother, Mary, and His earthly father, Joseph. Jesus became their son.

So even though Jesus is the Son of God, He was also born to earthly parents like we were. Mary and Joseph knew they were part of God's amazing, beautiful, and loving plan.

That night, instead of friends singing "Happy Birthday," the sky was filled with angels singing, "Glory to God in the highest"! Shepherds saw the angels and heard them singing praise to the baby Jesus.

The shepherds were really scared! But even in their fear, they hurried to see the newborn Son who was the Savior of the world. They wanted to see Christ the Lord, who would one day be nailed to a cross in the greatest act of love the world would ever know. The shepherds found the tiny new King and His exhausted parents, who were happy just to look at the One who had come to save them from their sin.

Mary and Joseph took care of their newborn son. They loved Him, fed Him, and sang to Him. They rocked Him to sleep, bathed Him, and kept Him warm. They did all the things a mommy and daddy do, because He was their son.

God didn't send Jesus to the earth inside a spaceship. Jesus didn't just suddenly appear when He was thirty years old. Jesus was born! He is the only one who is called the Son of God and the son of Mary and Joseph. Thank God that Jesus' birth was part of His incredible plan.

Dear Jesus, the Son of Mary and Joseph,

Thank You for coming into this world by being born to a young and trusting mother. You were raised in a family. You celebrated birthdays and special days. There was a day when You took Your first step and a day when You lost Your first tooth. You experienced so many things that I go through every day. Thank You for living a real life.

I pray in the name of Jesus, the son of Mary and Joseph, and the Son of God.

Amen.

> And Joseph also went up from Galilee, from the town of Nazareth, to Judea, to the city of David, which is called Bethlehem, because he was of the house and lineage of David, to be registered with Mary, his betrothed, who was with child. And while they were there, the time came for her to give birth. And she gave birth to her firstborn son and wrapped him in swaddling cloths and laid him in a manger, because there was no place for them in the inn.
> —Luke 2:4–7

Jesus is called...

The Son of Mary—Luke 2:48, Mark 6:3

Son of Joseph—Luke 4:22

Jesus Is God's Son

Maybe you are part of a team right now. Maybe it's a baseball team, a soccer team, a swim team, or a gymnastics team. If you aren't on a team now, you might be when you are older. And one day, on your way to a swim meet or a track meet, you might ask your parents, "If I win my race, will you be proud of me?"

Even though I won't be there, I think I know what your parents will say. They will probably say, "If you win your race, that would be really fun! But we are proud of you right now. You don't have to win anything for us to be proud. We love you just because you are you!" And when you hear wonderful words like that, it makes you feel special and loved.

Many children live with the same moms and dads who were there when they were born, and other kids live with just their mommy or just their daddy. Some are adopted into a forever family with a mommy and daddy who love them. Others may not live with their mommy and daddy right now but live with a foster family who takes care of them. Our parents love us. They take care of us and help us to grow. They are proud of us.

Jesus is God's eternal and forever Son. He was with God the Father when He created the world. And just like your parents have special names for you, God has a favorite name for Jesus—"My beloved Son." When Jesus was baptized by John the Baptist, a voice from heaven was heard saying, "You are my beloved Son; with you I am well pleased" (Mark 1:11).

We love when Mom and Dad say they are pleased with us after we have done a good job. We love to hear that they love us. When Jesus was baptized, He hadn't started the job God had sent Him to do on earth.

He hadn't yet done any teaching or miracles. He hadn't made the blind see or raised the dead. And most important, Jesus had not suffered and died on the cross. And yet, God told everyone that He loved His Son and was pleased with Him. Jesus didn't need to do anything to earn God's love. God loved Him and was pleased with Him just because Jesus was His.

Do you know God loves you and is pleased with you too? It's not because you are a really fast runner or get really good grades. It's not because you are super nice and have a lot of friends who trust you. It's not because you go to church every week or pray every day. Those things are all important, but the reason God loves you and is proud of you is because when you trust Jesus, you are His. You are a part of God's forever family. You are God's son or daughter, and you are beloved!

Dear Jesus, God's Beloved Son,

I know that right now, You love me and are proud of me. Just like Your Father was proud of You before You began Your work on earth, You are proud of me and love me, right where I am.

Help me to love You and obey You, not *so that* You will love me but *because* You love me. Every morning when I wake up, I pray the first thing I remember is that God loves me, God has adopted me into His forever family, and God is proud of me. Even though I am small, help me to remember this even when I am big.

I pray in the name of Jesus, the Son of God.
Amen.

> Jesus came from Nazareth of Galilee and was baptized by John in the Jordan. And when he came up out of the water, immediately he saw the heavens being torn open and the Spirit descending on him like a dove. And a voice came from heaven, "You are my beloved Son; with you I am well pleased."
> —Mark 1:9-11

Jesus is called...

The Son of God—John 11:4

My Beloved—Matthew 12:18

My Beloved Son—Matthew 17:5

Jesus Is a Teacher

Do you have a favorite teacher? Think about the wonderful things you love about that person. Why is that teacher special?

My favorite teacher made learning fun! She made it exciting to think about hard things. Some teachers would teach about butterflies by showing their students pictures in a book, but my teacher planted milkweed plants outside our classroom window. Then she took us outside and taught us about butterflies as we watched them flutter around the plants.

I loved how my teacher used creative ways to help me understand new things, even when the lesson was difficult. But most importantly, my teacher taught me that she loved me. Knowing you are genuinely loved by your teachers makes you want to be with them and learn from them.

Jesus may never have taught a classroom of children about butterflies, but He was known as "Teacher"! And He was one of those teachers who showed His students great love. His disciples loved being taught by Him, and they had so many questions. They wanted to know why Jesus taught by using stories. They wanted to understand why Jesus could do things they couldn't do. Once, when they thought they might drown, they asked Jesus if He even cared about them. They knew they could ask any question, especially when they were unsure of something. Jesus never made them feel silly for not knowing an answer.

Jesus was the perfect teacher, patiently showing His disciples new and wonderful things they had never heard before. He told them about who He was and about their heavenly Father. He taught everyone about His love. He taught them how to pray and how to love and treat others.

He helped them to understand they were broken with sin and needed to be rescued because they could not rescue themselves. He taught them that there was nothing they could do to make themselves good enough for heaven; instead, they needed to believe in Him.

Jesus teaches that you can't do enough good things to be loved by Him. You can't be perfect enough for Him to love you or to earn a ticket to go to heaven. But because God loves the world, He sent Jesus so that whoever believes in Him will live forever with God.

You need Jesus not only to be your teacher but also to be your rescuer. When you believe in Him, you ask Him to forgive your broken and messy heart. He teaches that you will live forever with Him.

Dear Jesus, the Perfect Teacher,

I'm thankful You teach me so many wonderful things about Yourself, Your Father, and the Holy Spirit. Thank You for teaching me how to live life in a way that brings glory to Your name.

Thank You for being patient with me, and please help me to be a better student. Help me to listen to Your Word, the Bible, and to love and learn from You more and more every day.

I pray in the name of Jesus, the greatest Teacher of all. Amen.

> Now there was a man of the Pharisees named Nicodemus, a ruler of the Jews. This man came to Jesus by night and said to him, "Rabbi, we know that you are a teacher come from God, for no one can do these signs that you do unless God is with him." —John 3:1–2

Jesus is called...

Teacher—Matthew 19:16

Good Teacher—Luke 18:18

Rabbi—Mark 9:5

Rabboni—John 20:16

Jesus Is God

What do you think is the strongest animal on earth? What about the most powerful machine or the smartest person? Earth holds some very powerful and strong things. And you're growing stronger and learning each day too! But no matter how strong and wise you become, there are many things you'll never be able to do. You will never create life from nothing. You will never give sight to the blind or raise someone from the dead. These most powerful and amazing things are only done by God.

Do you know the verse that says, "In the beginning, God created the heavens and the earth"? It's Genesis 1:1, the very first verse in the Bible. In the New Testament, the Gospel of John begins with a verse that sounds very similar. John 1:1–2 says, "In the beginning was the Word, and the Word was with God, and the Word was God. He was in the beginning with God."

When John talks about the "Word," this is another name for Jesus. The Bible tells us the Word was with God in the beginning. John also tells us that the Word was God. Jesus Christ is God. And that is the most wonderful news the world has ever heard.

While Jesus lived on earth, He was able to show the world that He was God. He healed people and raised them from the dead. He told His disciples that He too would die and rise from the dead in three days. And, most important of all, Jesus forgave people their sin. Only God can do that.

One day Jesus was teaching in a house that was so full of people that there wasn't enough room for everyone to get inside. Four men brought a crippled friend to be healed by Jesus. But the house was so crowded

that the only way the men could get their friend to Jesus was to break through the roof and lower their friend down using ropes. They hoped Jesus would heal their friend's body and believed their friend's biggest problem was that he couldn't walk. But Jesus knew that more than anything, the man needed his soul to be healed. So Jesus told the man that his sins were forgiven (Mark 2:5).

Several religious leaders were sitting and watching. When Jesus forgave the man's sins, the leaders grew angry with Jesus. They said that only God forgives sin. And they were right! The leaders just didn't know or believe that Jesus was God.

To make sure everyone knew the crippled man's sins were forgiven, Jesus also physically healed him. Because He is God, Jesus has all power, both to heal and to forgive.

When Jesus died on the cross, He forgave the sins of all the people who love and follow Him. He forgave your sins and the sins of your mommy and daddy. He forgave sin because Jesus Christ is God.

Dear Jesus, Who Is God,

I praise You that You are God! And because You are God, You forgive sin. Thank You for solving the biggest problem I will ever have in my life. Thank You for healing my sins and dying on a cross.

I want to live my life following Your directions. Help me, Jesus, to learn more about You every day. And help me to do what You want me to do every day.

I pray in the name of Jesus, my Lord and my God.
Amen.

Although the doors were locked, Jesus came and stood among them and said, "Peace be with you." Then he said to Thomas, "Put your finger here, and see my hands; and put out your hand, and place it in my side. Do not disbelieve, but believe." Thomas answered him, "My Lord and my God!" Jesus said to him, "Have you believed because you have seen me? Blessed are those who have not seen and yet have believed."
—John 20:26–29

Jesus is called…

Immanuel—Matthew 1:23

God—Luke 8:39   **The God of Israel**—Matthew 15:31

The Lamb of God—John 1:29

I AM, Ego Eimi—John 8:58   **The Word**—John 1:1, 14

The One Whom They Pierced—John 19:37

7
Jesus Is Lord

Have you noticed that some people have titles before their names? You call the person who does your health checkup "Doctor." The men and women who drive police cars and help us are called "Officers." The top firefighter is called "Chief." The person in charge of the army is called "General." The person who leads your church may be called "Pastor."

All those titles are special and tell us what that person does. But their titles are not their names.

Your doctor has a first name, such as Anne, and a last name, such as Williams. But when you see the doctor in her office, you might call her Doctor Williams. The title "Doctor" tells you about her job. She helps care for your body and keep it strong and healthy.

The police officer has a first name; it might be Todd. And he has a last name, such as Rodriguez. When you see him on the street, you might call him Officer Rodriguez. "Officer" tells us what he does at work. He protects you and helps keep you safe.

Jesus has a name that is a special title too. His name is Jesus, and His title is Lord. He is called Lord Jesus.

The name *Lord* tells us that Jesus has a special job. The title means He is in total control of all things. He is the master, the creator, the healer, and the forgiver. Because He is master, He can calm the roaring seas. Because He is Lord and Savior, He can calm the storms that rage in our hearts too.

In the Old Testament, God has a name and title too. His name is *Yahweh*, and His title is *Adonai*, which means Lord. When the Old Testament talks about Yahweh, it is written L{\sc ord} with all the letters capitalized. And when the Old Testament talks about the title of God, it is written *Lord*, with only the first letter capitalized. Sometimes, God's name and God's title are in the same verse, like Psalm 8:1.

It says, "O Lord, our Lord, how majestic is your name in all the earth!" The most important title for God in the Old Testament is *Lord*.

When you call Jesus Christ "Lord," you are saying He is God. This is important because only God can forgive sins.

Jesus didn't one day become Lord. He has always been Lord. Before He came to earth, He was Lord. And on the day He was born in Bethlehem, He was Lord. When the angels lit up the skies and appeared to the shepherds on the glorious night of Jesus' birth, they announced, "For unto you is born this day in the city of David a Savior, who is Christ the Lord" (Luke 2:11). And just like the angels worshipped Jesus the Lord, God wants everyone to worship Jesus as Lord. The Bible tells us that all people who say with their mouths that Jesus Christ is Lord and believe in their hearts that God raised Him from the dead will be saved (Romans 10:9).

Like with doctors and police officers, Jesus' title also tells us about His job, except His job was a really big one. The Lord Jesus took all our sin and brokenness on Himself when He went to the cross. Our Lord Jesus died the death we deserved. And the Lord Jesus showed us why He deserves to be called Lord: He defeated death by rising from the grave.

Dear Lord Jesus,

You are in control of all things. Because You are Lord, only You can help my heart love You more every day.

In the days when You were on earth, the biggest ruler of the land wanted to be lord. I know that even now many people and many things want to be the lord of my life and control it. Help me never to allow anyone or anything to take the place of You as Lord of my heart. Help me today to worship only You as Lord.

Please be the Lord of my heart and my hands. Be Lord over everything in my life.

I pray in the name of the Lord Jesus.
Amen.

> For unto you is born this day in the city of David a Savior, who is Christ the Lord.
> —Luke 2:11

Jesus is called...

Lord Jesus—Mark 16:19

The Lord—Luke 19:31

Lord of the Harvest—Matthew 9:38

Lord of the Sabbath—Luke 6:5

My Lord and My God—John 20:28

He Who Comes in the Name of the Lord—Mark 11:9

Jesus Is the Christ

It's fun to win! Crossing the finish line first in a race is an amazing feeling. Or being the last speller standing at the school spelling bee, or being the fastest swimmer at your neighborhood pool, or winning the Little League championship. When you work hard and get rewarded, it feels very special.

When you win, you get to be called a champion. But did you know there's another kind of champion? A champion can be a person who cares for you, a person who loves you and protects you. If a bully is mean to you, and a friend defends you and tells the bully to stop, that friend is your champion.

Can you remember what we talked about in the last chapter? We talked about how some people have titles before their names. We talked about how *Jesus* is a name and *Lord* is a title. Let's talk about another title of Jesus. Jesus was also called *Christ*. Sometimes our Lord is called Jesus Christ. Other times we use two titles when we call him our *Lord Jesus Christ*.

In the Old Testament, God promised His chosen people that a Messiah would one day come to deliver them from their sins. In the New Testament, instead of using the title *Messiah* we use the title *Christ*. When we call Jesus by the name *Christ*, we are saying that Jesus is our Messiah, which is another word for champion. It means that God chose Jesus to be the Anointed One who would save us from our sins. We are saying that Jesus is the perfect prophet, the perfect priest, and the perfect king. That's a lot to understand, but just remember we are saying that Jesus is everything!

Let's try to put this all together. Sometimes you might call Jesus, *My Lord and Savior Jesus Christ*. That is a supreme name! When you put all of those titles together, you are saying so much! You are saying that Jesus is in control. You are saying He is your Defender and Savior. You are saying He is your Champion. You are declaring that Jesus is your Healer and the One who forgives you. You are  announcing He is the Master and Creator who holds the entire universe together. Wow!

Now, here is the really, *really* good news. When you say Jesus is all those things, you are also admitting you don't need to be those things. Sure, you still might want to be a sports champion or a spelling bee champion, but you don't need to be the champion of your family. Jesus already has that job. And you don't need to be the savior. Jesus has that job too! You don't need to worry about filling the job of healing broken hearts and broken families. Jesus is working on that every second of every minute of every hour of every day.

Jesus never stops being the Messiah. He never, not even for one minute, stops being your Champion. He is always your Savior. Your mommy and daddy might have days when they don't have to go to work, but Jesus goes to work every day. He never stops being the Christ.

What is the very best way to show that Jesus is the Christ? Let Him love you. Enjoy all the goodness that your champion, the Lord Jesus Christ, has for you today.

Dear Jesus the Christ,

You are my Champion! I love You. Thank You for being the Messiah who died on the cross to forgive me of my sins.

I know that many people in this world believe You are only a great teacher and a strong leader. Jesus, I want them to believe You are so much more. Please help their hearts to believe that You are the Messiah! You are the Christ who has come to forgive us of our sins and be our Champion.

Help me and my parents to sleep well tonight knowing You are the Champion of our family.

I pray in the name of my Lord and Savior Jesus Christ.

Amen.

> **Simon Peter replied, "You are the Christ, the Son of the living God."**
> **—Matthew 16:16**

Jesus is called...

The Christ—Matthew 26:63, Mark 8:29, John 11:27

Jesus Christ—Mark 1:1, John 1:17

The Christ of God—Luke 9:20

Messiah the Christ—John 1:41

Jesus Is King

I love stories about kings, queens, princesses, and knights in shining armor. In these stories, kings are often the most powerful rulers of all. They live in majestic castles and wear long robes covered in expensive jewels. Their crowns are crafted from gold and heavy with diamonds, rubies, and precious stones. Sometimes the king carries a scepter too. And when he passes by his people, they kneel at his feet because he is the mighty ruler.

Jesus is called *King* in the Bible. People might think that while Jesus was on earth He should have worn a crown, carried a scepter, and lived in a royal palace. Others might think He should have controlled huge armies of soldiers.

After all, God's people had been waiting for a king like that to come save them. Some were expecting the king to ride into their city on a majestic white horse swinging a golden sword. They hoped this king would destroy the rulers who had been so horribly mean for so terribly long. People thought the king would be a rich, strong, and powerful leader who could put an end to all their suffering. But Jesus wasn't this kind of king at all.

People thought their king should be born in Jerusalem, where there were many Roman palaces. But Jesus was born in Bethlehem, a sleepy village filled with farms, gardens, and herds of animals. Kings should be born in a beautiful room surrounded by the best doctors and nurses.

But Jesus was most likely born in a dirty room surrounded by animals and welcomed by homeless shepherds. Jesus didn't look like the expected king.

So when Jesus became a grown man and walked among these same people, they did not recognize Him as King. He was not dressed in a fancy robe, and He did not wear a crown. But Jesus was still the King God had promised would come to rescue His people from their sin.

Jesus was indeed the most powerful person in the world, but He got down on His knees and washed the feet of His disciples. Jesus was the King of kings and Lord of lords, yet He made breakfast for His disciples. Jesus showed the people what true love looked like. He healed the sick, helped the poor, and taught everyone about God's love. Jesus was a very different King!

The people who didn't believe He was their King had Him killed on the cross. When Jesus rose three days later, He showed the people that He was King even over death!

One day Jesus will come back. Trumpets will sound, the skies will open, and all people will see King Jesus riding on a horse. Every knee will bow. All people will know that Jesus is King. Those who love Jesus will get to live in His forever kingdom, where He will forever reign as King of all!

> Then Pilate said to him, "So you are a king?" Jesus answered, "You say that I am a king. For this purpose I was born and for this purpose I have come into the world—to bear witness to the truth. Everyone who is of the truth listens to my voice."—John 18:37

Dear King Jesus,

Thank You for being a King who loves, serves, and cares for Your people. Even though You are a King, thank You for coming into this world in humility. Thank You for loving the poor and spending time with children. Thank You for being a different kind of King.

I admit there are days when I want to be king. There are times when I want to be the ruler of my life. But I know that will only lead to hurt and pain. Help me to live my life under Your rule instead. Help me to always bow my knee to You, every day of my life.

I pray in the name of Jesus, my King. Amen.

Jesus is called...

King—Matthew 21:5, Luke 19:38

King of the Jews—Matthew 2:2, Mark 15:26

King of Israel—John 1:49

Ruler—Matthew 2:6

Someone Greater than Solomon—Matthew 12:41

Jesus Is the Holy One

Have you ever seen something so beautiful that you stop whatever you are doing and take in a deep breath? When seeing something stunning, some people like to say it takes their breath away. Maybe it is a gorgeous butterfly. Maybe it is a majestic rainbow over the ocean or a shooting star streaking across the sky.

Whatever it is, you know it is something amazing. The big ending of a fireworks show, a brand-new baby brother or sister, or a puppy licking your face. All these things might leave you feeling like you can't find words to say how beautiful they are.

Or maybe you see something so scary it takes your breath away! Maybe it is a slithering snake, a hailstorm, or a really big spider! When something takes your breath away, and you can't find the right words, you might pull on Mom or Dad's arm to get them to look at it too.

God's holiness can take our breath away. I remember one morning talking to my students about the holiness of God, when one little girl said, "It is like seeing the bright morning sun with all the pretty colors in the sky and saying, 'Ahhh'!"

What does it mean that something is holy? Holiness is very hard to describe. When people in the Bible saw the holiness of God, they would fall to their knees. They were not able to speak. They were at times frightened. In the Old Testament, Isaiah tells us about seeing the holiness of God. He said that holy, holy, holy is the never-ending song of praise that is being sung around the throne of God right now! He cried out, "Woe is me! For I am lost!" because he was an unclean sinner standing in the presence of the one and only holy and perfect God (Isaiah 6:5).

Holiness is both beautiful and overwhelming. Jesus was both, so one of His names is *Holy*, just like God.

God is holy. When Adam and Eve sinned in the garden of Eden, they became unholy. God had to send them away because He cannot look at anything sinful. And because of our sinful hearts, we too are not holy. The Bible says that sinful hearts deserve death (Romans 6:23). That sounds like really sad news. We cannot be with God if we are sinful and unholy.

But there is wonderful, life-changing news! Jesus is the Holy One of God. Jesus came to this earth so that you could be made right with God. And because Jesus, who lived a perfect and sinless and holy life, is your representative before God the Father, you too are declared holy! The Bible tells you that as an obedient child of God, you need to be holy in all you say and do (1 Peter 1:14–16). That is only possible because of Jesus. God has given us such a wonderful gift of holiness that it takes our breath away!

Dear Jesus, the Holy One of God,

Thank You for being holy. Thank You for living a holy life. When I think about Your holiness and the way You lived a perfectly obedient life, it takes my breath away.

Jesus, I struggle to live a life of holiness. Every day I find it hard to obey You. Help me live in a way that reflects Your holiness to my family, my friends, and all those I see every day. May people around me be amazed, not at what they see in me, but at Your holiness reflected through me. Help me to live as a forgiven and changed child of the King of kings and Lord of lords, the Holy One of God.

I pray in the name of Jesus, the Holy One sent by God.
Amen.

> And immediately there was in their synagogue a man with an unclean spirit. And he cried out, "What have you to do with us, Jesus of Nazareth? Have you come to destroy us? I know who you are—the Holy One of God."
> —Mark 1:23-24

Jesus is called...

Holy—Luke 1:35

The Holy One of God—Mark 1:24, Luke 4:34, John 6:69

Jesus Is a Friend

Everyone needs friends. They are a sweet gift. Some of us have a lot of friends, and some of us just have one or two. Our friends are the ones we love to play with, tell our secrets to, or hug when we are feeling sad. Friends remind us that no one was meant to be alone. It's a good feeling when someone calls you "friend."

Our human friends aren't perfect, though, are they? Sometimes best friends hurt our feelings when they don't choose us for their team at recess. Sometimes our friends choose to play with somebody else. Sometimes our friends don't share. They can even say something that really hurts our hearts.

When your friends hurt your feelings, sometimes you might get really mad and say mean things to them. Sometimes you might ignore them and act like they aren't your friends anymore. Sometimes you might just cry.

Like you, Jesus had friends. He was called "friend" too. And sometimes those relationships made Him sad. The disciples were Jesus' best friends. They went everywhere with Him. They ate with Him, talked with Him, laughed with Him, and learned all about Him. They loved Jesus, and Jesus loved them.

But on the saddest day, the day when Jesus was taken away to die on the cross, some of Jesus' friends ran away. They were scared. They didn't understand what God was doing. Later, when Peter, who was one of Jesus' very best friends, was asked if he knew Jesus, he said he didn't even know who Jesus was. Can you imagine how hurt you would be if your friends acted like they didn't know you?

The greatest day ever was when Jesus rose from the grave, showing everyone He has power over death. Then He went to see His disciples. Can you imagine how surprised and happy they all were to see Him? The Bible tells us they were scared at first (Luke 24:37). But Jesus let them touch Him so that they would know He really was alive.

One morning a few days later, seven of the disciples went fishing (John 21:1–14). Jesus was standing on the shore, but the disciples didn't know it was Him. They hadn't caught any fish. Then Jesus told them to throw their nets on the other side of the boat. When they did, they caught so many fish! Suddenly they knew the man on the shore was Jesus. They hurried and brought the fish to Jesus. Do you know what Jesus did then? He made them breakfast.

Jesus showed His friends they were forgiven for running away from Him. He loved His friends. I'll bet that breakfast was the best one those seven friends ever had as they got to talk and laugh and be with Jesus. Most importantly, they realized that their best friend Jesus had conquered death!

Jesus is your best friend too. When you make mistakes, He still loves you. He has proven that He will never turn His back on you. He loves, forgives, and shows you what it looks like to be a truly great friend.

Dear Jesus, my Friend,

Thank You for being the most faithful friend ever! Thank You for promising to always love me with an everlasting love. Thank You for loving Your disciples, even after they had run away from You when You needed them the most.

I confess that I am a sinner. Sometimes I do things that are wrong. Thank You for being a forgiving friend who will never abandon me, even when I sin.

Help me today to be a better friend. Help me to be a kind, forgiving, and always loving friend, even when others might hurt my feelings.

I pray in the name of my Friend, Jesus.

Amen.

> "This is my commandment, that you love one another as I have loved you. Greater love has no one than this, that someone lay down his life for his friends. You are my friends if you do what I command you. No longer do I call you servants, for the servant does not know what his master is doing; but I have called you friends, for all that I have heard from my Father I have made known to you."
> —John 15:12–15

Jesus is called...

Friend of Tax Collectors and Sinners—Luke 7:34

12
Jesus Is the Great I AM

Emotions can be confusing. One minute we're laughing, and the next minute we feel angry. Can you remember the last time you felt really happy? When was the last time you were scared? How about the last time you cried? When were you last surprised? That's a fun emotion when it's a surprise party on your birthday! But it's not much fun when you're surprised by a loud BOOM of thunder that rattles your window.

Did you know that Jesus feels emotions? He feels love for His followers, and He celebrates when we repent of our sins. But as He sits next to God the Father in heaven, there is one emotion Jesus never experiences. Jesus is never surprised. He is never caught off guard. Jesus never experiences surprise, because He is sovereign, He is God, and He has a perfect plan.

Sovereign is a big and very important word that means having power over everything. It's like being the boss of the whole world. Jesus has more power than the rulers of our country. He has more control than kings and queens around the world. He has power over sicknesses. And most important, He has power over life and death.

When the Bible says Jesus is sovereign over everything, it means Jesus has all things under His control, even the things that are scary to you. You may be afraid of snakes and spiders. You may be scared of the dark. You may be very afraid of big thunderstorms and find yourself creeping into Mommy and Daddy's bed after that super-loud thunderclap! Jesus being sovereign means that even during hurricanes, tornadoes, scary fires, and uncertain days, Jesus has everything under control.

Jesus says several important things about Himself to tell us He is sovereign and He is God. In the Gospel of John, Jesus makes eight statements that begin with the words, "I am." These are some of His magnificent names. We will talk about every one of these names in later chapters.

Read these statements slowly and think about how each one says something important about Jesus. Jesus said:

"I am the bread of life." "I am the light of the world."
"I am the door of the sheep." "I am the good shepherd."
"I am the resurrection and the life." "I am the true vine."
"I am the way, the truth, and the life."

Jesus said the eighth and maybe the most important "I am" statement after He told a crowd of people that He had seen Abraham (John 8:58). This seemed silly to the people listening. Abraham had been dead for hundreds of years!

Jesus told the people that before Abraham was even born, "I am." When Jesus said, "I am," He said it in a really funny way. He used a Greek phrase that literally means, "I I I am." That's right. Jesus said "I" three times! Here is why that is so important: God the Father had called Himself this exact same name when He appeared in the burning bush to Moses many, many years earlier (Exodus 3:14). When Moses asked God His name, God said, "I I I am." When Jesus said, "I I I am," He was saying He had always existed. He was telling the people He was God. This made the people so mad. Some people even picked up rocks to throw at Jesus because they did not believe Him!

But Jesus wanted the people, and us, to know the "I am" part of His name. "I am" is a reminder that Jesus is sovereign over everything. Even the scary and surprising things. He has power over it all. He is the great "I am," He is God, and He is in control.

You can sleep well tonight. God's got this!

Dear Jesus, the Great I AM,

Thank You for being sovereign. Thank You for using Your power and Your authority for good.

Forgive me when I think that my plan is better than Your plan. I ask that You help me believe that Your ways are always the very best.

Please help me to sleep soundly every night knowing that You are in control. While I am asleep tonight, You will not be asleep. You will once again be up all night, sovereignly holding everything together. Help me to sleep because You have a perfect plan.

I pray in the name of Jesus, the Great I AM. Amen.

Jesus said to them, "Truly, truly, I say to you, before Abraham was, I am."
—John 8:58

Jesus calls Himself...

"I am the bread of life."—John 6:35

"I am the light of the world."—John 8:12

"I am the door of the sheep."—John 10:7

"I am the resurrection and the life."—John 11:25

"I am the good shepherd."—John 10:11

"I am the way, and the truth, and the life."—John 14:6

"I am the true vine."—John 15:1   "I am."—John 8:58

Jesus Is God's Chosen

We all love to be chosen.

It's fun to be chosen to be on someone's team. It makes you feel good inside when you hear your name called to join a game on the playground. It means someone wants to be with you. Somebody is choosing you to do something special.

It makes us feel unique when we are singled out and chosen to help with something at home too. You might know that feeling, especially if you have other brothers and sisters. Doesn't it feel good when Mom or Dad chooses you to be the one to run an errand alone with them or to help with a special project?

Being chosen makes us feel very special and reminds us we are being noticed. It creates a wonderful feeling deep inside our bones that tells us we are one of a kind. It's like someone saying, "There is no one else like you!"

Here is some really fun news. God chose you! God chose you to be you, and nobody else. God chose you to be unique. The Bible says you are God's masterpiece (Ephesians 2:10). He individually created you to be unlike anyone else in the entire world. You are one of a kind!

Jesus knows what it's like to be chosen too. In fact, one of His names is the "Chosen One." He is called that because He is the only One in the entire world who could do a very special job. In fact, the job Jesus did was the most important thing that anyone has been chosen to do—*ever*!

Your parents probably have a lot of names for you. Maybe they call you "Princess" or "Buddy." Maybe they call you "Champ" or "Baby." When parents use different names, it's just another way to say they love you.

God has a lot of names for His Son, Jesus. God calls Him "My Chosen One." He also calls Him "My Messenger," "My Servant," "My Beloved Son," and "My Sent." Did you notice all those names start with the word *My*? We often say things like, "That is *MY* toy." Or "That is *MY* room." We use the word *my* to let others know what belongs to us.

When God says, "My," He is saying that Jesus is His! Jesus is *His* Chosen One.

Before Jesus had performed any miracles or asked twelve men to become His disciples, John the Baptist was telling people about Jesus. John described Him by saying, "This is God's Chosen One" (John 1:34 NIV).

Do you want to know how much God loves you? Think about this: God sent His One and only Chosen Son to earth to serve us, to teach us, and to love us. Most importantly, God sent His Chosen One to die for us so that we might live forever with the God who created us and loves us and chooses us.

Dear Jesus, the Chosen One,

God chose You to do the most important job ever, to be His messenger and His servant. Before the beginning of time, You were chosen to be God's Son. And You chose to die on a cross so that I could be chosen to live!

Jesus, thank You for choosing to create me to be unlike anyone else. Thank You for choosing me to be on Your team. Thank You for giving Your life so that we could live together forever.

Help me today to live my life as a son or daughter of the King of kings and Lord of lords! I am chosen!

I pray in the name of Jesus, God's Chosen One.
Amen.

> "I myself [John the Baptist] did not know him, but he who sent me to baptize with water said to me, 'He on whom you see the Spirit descend and remain, this is he who baptizes with the Holy Spirit.' And I have seen and have borne witness that this is the Son of God." —John 1:33–34

Jesus is called...

My Chosen One—Luke 9:35

My Messenger—Matthew 11:10

My Servant—Matthew 12:18   **My Sent**—John 5:38

My Beloved Son—Matthew 17:5

Jesus Is the Light

Have you ever been in a really dark hiding place? The kind of place where it was so dark you couldn't even see your fingers? Or maybe you have gone on a field trip or vacation and walked through a cave where there wasn't any light.

At night, after Mommy and Daddy turn out your light, does your room get super dark? Sometimes being in the dark is really scary. Maybe you like to pull the covers up over your head.

Once in a while the darkness may frighten us enough that we call out for someone to come save us. What happens as soon as Mommy or Daddy arrive and turn on the light? The darkness disappears. The light takes over all the darkness, and suddenly you can see the entire room.

It's nice to have the lights back on so that we are not afraid anymore. But with the lights on, we can also see *everything* in our rooms—the toys we didn't put away, the dust on the dresser, and that pile of markers and paper and glue sticks that now makes our room look messy. The light shines on what is beautiful, but it also shows us the things that are dirty.

When you think about how much power light has, it's no surprise that one of Jesus' names is "the Light." When the darkness is scary, He can comfort us so that we don't have to be afraid. When we have a big decision to make and aren't sure which way to go, Jesus lights our path and shows us the way.

His light also shines on the messy things in our heart—the grudges, the grumpiness, the guilt. Shining a light on those yucky things usually makes us feel uncomfortable, but Jesus knows we need to see them! We need His Light to show us the yuck and sin so that we can ask Him to forgive us and clean up the messy things in our heart.

In the book of John, Jesus says, "I am the light of the world" (John 8:12). He says if we follow Him, we will not walk in the darkness. Now, that doesn't mean your room won't still be dark sometimes. But it does mean that Jesus will continue to comfort you when you're scared and will shine on the places of your heart that need His light.

And just like in your bedroom when you turn on the lights, His light covers all the darkness in your heart until you can see everything.

Jesus is the Light! He is bigger than the darkest things of this world. We need the Light of the World to save us from darkness and from the messy things cluttering up our hearts.

Here is something else amazing about Jesus being the Light of the World—He shares His Light with everyone who loves Him. In Matthew 5, Jesus preaches a message we call the Sermon on the Mount. In that message, He says *you* are the light of the world (v. 14). When you love Jesus, He says you can be a light for Him in a dark world. How cool is that? Let His light shine!

Dear Jesus, the Light of the World,

You are the Light of my heart. Protect me from the dark and scary things of this world. I know Your light is bigger than the darkest of dark places. I know Your light is all I need to show me the dark places of my heart.

Please forgive me, Jesus, for the messy things in my heart. And thank You for being the Light that overcomes all the darkness in my life. Help me be a bright light that shines in a dark world that needs You.

I pray in the name of Jesus, the Light of the World.
Amen

> Again Jesus spoke to them, saying, "I am the light of the world. Whoever follows me will not walk in darkness, but will have the light of life."
> —John 8:12

Jesus is called...

The Light—John 1:5, John 12:35–36

The True Light—John 1:9

Great Light—Matthew 4:16

Light of the World—John 8:12

The Light of Men—John 1:4

Jesus Is the Bread of Life

A long time ago, someone mixed flour and water and put it in some sort of oven where it was surrounded by heat. And poof! Bread was invented! I'm guessing you like to eat bread. Maybe you like bread in the form of a hamburger bun. If you are like me, you like bread covered with peanut butter and jelly and eaten at a picnic with friends! Maybe a grilled cheese sandwich is your favorite. Or maybe you like a hot dinner roll just out of the oven. There are so many different kinds of bread! The wonderful thing about bread is it tastes yummy and takes away our hunger.

I'm pretty sure you were able to eat something for dinner last night. And you probably ate something for breakfast and lunch today. Maybe your meals included bread. You know what it feels like to have your tummy growl because you are hungry, and you also know the feeling of your tummy being full and happy. We call that being satisfied.

There is nothing like coming home after a day at school or waking up from a nap and smelling something yummy in the kitchen. One of my favorites is warm chocolate chip cookies right out of the oven. They are even better with a glass of ice-cold milk—yummy and satisfying!

Sadly, many children around the world haven't eaten anything today. It makes me so sad, but some children haven't eaten for several days. These children know what it is like not only to be hungry but also to be starving. When someone doesn't eat for a very long time, they are starving. Many of us don't know what that feels like.

In the book of Exodus in the Old Testament, we read the story of the Israelites, God's chosen people, as they wandered through the desert in search of the new home God had promised them. When the traveling Israelites grew very hungry, God took great care of them by sending bread to fall from the sky every morning for the people to gather. The Bible calls the bread "manna" (Exodus 16:31). It was just what the people needed to satisfy their tummies.

We have a hunger that is deeper than the hunger we feel in our tummies. There is a longing deep in our hearts that can't be filled by the bread your parents might buy at the store or make at home. It can't be filled by toys. It can't be satisfied by a better bike. We have a need that can't be filled by more building sets or a new doll. Our deep need can't be met by having lots of friends. It is a hunger that can only be filled by Jesus.

One of Jesus' names is the "Bread of Life." It's a wonderful reminder that only loving and trusting Jesus, the Bread of Life, can truly satisfy us. He is the Bread that God sent us from heaven, like the way God sent the manna down from heaven for the Israelites. Jesus is the Bread that satisfies us deeper than our bellies. He fills the hunger deep in our hearts too.

Dear Jesus, the Bread of Life,

Thank You for giving my family bread to eat. I pray that You will provide bread for the children around the world who need food to grow and be healthy.

Thank You that You are the Bread that came down from heaven. You are the only one who can satisfy my deepest hunger, a hunger that goes way deeper than the hunger in my belly.

I confess that I often think I need more stuff to feel full and satisfied. I want more toys, bigger toys, and better toys. But the deep hunger I have in my heart can't be filled by any stuff. It can only be filled by You.

Every time I take a bite of bread, remind me that You are the Bread of Life. Remind me that You alone can satisfy me, that only You can fill my heart-hunger.

I pray in the name of Jesus, the Bread of Life.
Amen.

> Jesus said to them, "I am the bread of life; whoever comes to me shall not hunger, and whoever believes in me shall never thirst."
> —John 6:35

Jesus is called...

The Bread of Life—John 6:35

The Bread that Came Down from Heaven—John 6:41

The Living Bread—John 6:51

Jesus Is Living Water

Imagine it's a super-hot summer day. You've been playing outside for hours. There isn't much shade, and the swimming pool is closed. Mom says you can't turn on the sprinkler, and your friend just had you chase her in a game of "Catch Me if You Can." You are trying to catch your breath, but it's hard because your mouth is so dry. You run inside. What's the first thing you do?

Did you say water? Of course! You would be so thirsty that all you can think of is a nice, cold glass of water. Think how it feels drinking it down. Your thirst is quenched. Your body begins to cool off. You can catch your breath and may feel ready to go back outside and chase your friend all over again.

That's what water does. It refreshes your body. You can feel it all the way deep inside. When you are hot and tired, nothing refreshes you like a tall glass of ice-cold water. You are probably thirsty right now just thinking about it!

Speaking of water, did you know that Jesus is called Living Water?

When Jesus walked on the earth, there were no drinking fountains. There were only wells. A thirsty person would lower a bucket attached to a rope into a deep well and pull up the water. It was a lot of work to get a drink!

In one story in the Gospel of John, Jesus meets a woman at a well (John 4). He asks her for a drink, and they begin to talk. Jesus tells her that everyone will always be thirsty for water and that everyone who drinks water will soon be thirsty again. But the water that Jesus gives is Living Water. If we drink that water, we will never be thirsty again!

Jesus talks about Living Water again when He is standing in front of the angry Pharisees and officers who want to arrest Him. He says everyone who believes in Jesus will have the Living Water flow from their hearts. Jesus is talking about the Holy Spirit.

Water quenches our thirst for a while, but we will get thirsty again. But when we believe in Jesus and our hearts are filled with Living Water, the thirst of our hearts and souls will be quenched. We will never be thirsty again. Jesus quenches the deepest thirstiness of our souls. We were made to need Jesus and long for Him. We were created to be thirsty for Jesus.

Jesus teaches His followers that when we love Him, we are the salt of the earth (Matthew 5:13). Do you know what salt does? It makes people thirsty. Isn't that awesome? We are given the job of making people thirsty for Jesus, and Jesus is the Living Water that can satisfy their thirst. How perfect is that?

Dear Jesus, the Water of Life,

Thank You for being the only One who can satisfy my deepest thirst. Only You can refresh me.

You once stood in the middle of a large crowd and said, "If anyone thirsts, let him come to me and drink" (John 7:37). We live in a thirsty world. So many of the world's problems would look different if people would only come to You and drink. Help more people know they are thirsty and realize that You are the only One who can satisfy their thirst.

Jesus, my Living Water, help me tell others about You. Help me to live as the salt of the earth. Make me Your "salty" follower, making those around me thirsty for You too.

I pray in the name of Jesus, the Living Water.
Amen.

> Jesus said to her, "Everyone who drinks of this water will be thirsty again, but whoever drinks of the water that I will give him will never be thirsty again. The water that I will give him will become in him a spring of water welling up to eternal life."
> —John 4:13–14

Jesus is called...

The Living Water—John 7:37–39

Jesus Is the Prophet

Let's imagine I have a tall jar filled with a hundred beautiful, colorful marbles. There are blue marbles, yellow marbles, and multi-colored marbles. Some marbles are purple, white, and green. But there is only one bright red marble in the jar. Now, suppose you closed your eyes, stuck your hand into the jar, and pulled out just one marble. If you really kept your eyes shut, do you think you could choose the red marble? If you did, it would be amazing!

Now picture this. A swimming pool is filled with marbles. And again, there is just one red marble. If your eyes were closed, could you pick out the red marble? It seems like it would be almost impossible.

Have you ever seen pictures of the Grand Canyon? It is a giant, spectacular hole in the ground that was created by God a long, long time ago. What if you were to fill the Grand Canyon with trillions and trillions of marbles—but just one red marble. If you were to pick out the red marble, it would be a miracle!

In the Old Testament, God gave us prophets to point to the coming of Jesus. Maybe you have heard some of their names. Elijah, Elisha, Miriam, Micah, Jonah, Deborah, Isaiah, Jeremiah, Ezekiel, and Hosea are just a few of the prophets sent by God. God allowed them to look into the future and see the coming Messiah. Many of them wrote down what they saw.

The prophets saw the Messiah's birth. They knew He would be born in Bethlehem to a virgin. They knew one of Jesus' friends would betray Him for thirty pieces of silver. They saw that Jesus would die on a cross next to criminals. God allowed the prophets to see hundreds of things about Jesus, all hundreds of years before He came to earth!

Here is the amazing thing. Jesus perfectly fulfilled every prophecy. It would be like filling all of outer space with marbles. Think about it. Marbles would surround the sun, the planets, and every star you can see at night, and even those you can't see. Every space, everywhere, would be filled with marbles. Could anyone pick out the one red marble, with their eyes closed, on their first try? To think about someone doing that is just plain silly!

But God could do it! He sent Jesus, who perfectly fulfilled every prophecy. Every single one! It's like He picked out the one red marble!

The Bible tells us that all the prophets pointed to Jesus, the perfect Prophet. Now Jesus can point to Himself and say that He is the One who has fulfilled everything to which the prophets pointed. Jesus is the Prophet sent by God to testify to Himself. He is the complete and final fulfillment of all the Bible's promises!

And for Jesus to fulfill everything the prophets said about Him ... well, that's a red-marble miracle!

Dear Jesus, the Greatest Prophet,

You were sent by Your heavenly Father to earth to love me, give Your life for me, and forgive me of my sins.

I'm grateful I can know the Bible is true. Thank You for sending prophets to point to You, the perfect Prophet. Thank You that everything the prophets said about You, Jesus, came true. It is like picking out the one red marble from a universe filled with marbles. It is a miracle! Jesus, You are a miracle.

Help me to have greater trust that the Bible is true. Thank You that Your truth is bigger than any doubts I might have right now or at any time in my life.

I pray in the name of Jesus, the Prophet sent by God.
Amen.

And the crowds that went before him and that followed him were shouting, "Hosanna to the Son of David! Blessed is he who comes in the name of the Lord! Hosanna in the highest!" And when he entered Jerusalem, the whole city was stirred up, saying, "Who is this?" And the crowds said, "This is the prophet Jesus, from Nazareth of Galilee."
—Matthew 21:9–11

Jesus is called...

Prophet—John 4:19, John 9:17

The Prophet Jesus—Matthew 21:11

The Prophet Who Has Come into the World—John 6:14

Prophet Mighty in Word and Deed Before All the People—Luke 24:19

One of the Prophets of Old—Luke 9:19   **Elijah**—Luke 9:19

Someone Greater than Jonah—Matthew 12:41

Jesus Is the Horn of Salvation

Have you ever seen someone be rescued? Maybe you were playing a game of capture the flag, and someone was rescued from the other team's jail. Or perhaps a toddler was standing too close to the edge of the pool or a tall building and a parent pulled him away from danger. Or maybe you've seen a cat being rescued from a tree!

A lot of books and movies are about someone who needs help. Maybe it is a story about a princess who is saved by a brave prince. Maybe it is an animal who needs to be protected and saved when caught in a giant blizzard. Many of the most loved stories are about someone who needs to be rescued. Do you know why? Because deep in our hearts, we know that we need to be rescued too.

Did you know that everyone who loves the Lord Jesus Christ has been rescued? God's rescue of His people is a beautiful story of never-ending love and powerful grace. We were saved by Jesus, the Horn of Salvation.

When you hear that one of Jesus' names is the Horn of Salvation, maybe you think of a bicycle horn or a car horn. You might think about a horn like a trumpet or trombone. But when Jesus is called the Horn of Salvation, it is a different kind of horn.

Have you ever seen a cow or a sheep with big horns? When the Bible says that Jesus is the Horn of Salvation, it is saying that Jesus is like the horns of a wild ox, which is bigger and stronger than a cow. The ox horn was blown in battle to alert soldiers. It was so strong that it was nearly impossible to break. The horn of a wild ox could also be used as a weapon.

When King David wrote Psalm 18, the Lord had just rescued him from Saul and his armies. David gave thanks to the Lord for saving him and wrote, "The LORD is my rock and my fortress and my deliverer, my God, my rock in whom I take refuge, my shield, and the horn of my salvation."

David's words tell us a great deal about God. He is stable and unmoving like a rock. He is strong and powerful like a fortress. He is brave like a rescuer. He is protective like a shield, and He is mighty like a horn. Everything that David wrote about pointed to Jesus.

Just like the way God rescued David from his enemies, Jesus has rescued you. The Creator of the universe, the King above all kings, the Lord who is over everything, He went to battle to win you, make you free, and save you. We know that God was fighting the armies of Saul to rescue David. But who is Jesus fighting to rescue you?

Jesus fought the battle against darkness and death. He fought Satan, who is a liar, a thief, and a destroyer of good (John 10:10). Jesus, the Horn of Salvation, fought against the evil one by willingly giving His life on the cross. When Jesus died, Satan thought he had won! He thought he had defeated the Horn of Salvation. But early in the morning, on the third day after He had been buried, Jesus conquered death by rising from the grave. He did it all to rescue you. This is your story. And there is no greater story.

Think about that. You are worth fighting for. God battled to secure and protect everyone who calls His name. Thank God for sending Jesus, the Horn of Salvation.

Dear Jesus, the Horn of my Salvation,

Thank You for loving me so much that You went to battle for me. You fought so that I would be rescued from death. I know the only way You could defeat death and save me was by willingly giving Your own life. And when You did that, You rescued me.

I praise You that You defeated both death and the grave by Your death and resurrection. Help me today to know that You are my Rock, my Fortress, my Deliverer, and my Protector. You are my Salvation.

I pray in the name of Jesus, my Rescuer.
Amen.

> And his father Zechariah was filled with the Holy Spirit and prophesied, saying, "Blessed be the Lord God of Israel, for he has visited and redeemed his people and has raised up a horn of salvation for us in the house of his servant David."
> —Luke 1:67–69

Jesus is called...

A Horn of Salvation—Luke 1:69

The Lord's Salvation—Luke 2:30

Jesus Is the One Who Came Down from Heaven

What do we celebrate at Christmas? Three simple words. *God came down.* Now, this doesn't mean that God just fell down from the sky like manna or snowflakes, only to melt and disappear the next day. No, when God came down to earth in the person of Jesus, the world forever changed.

In a letter to a church, Paul wrote that when Jesus came to this earth, He emptied Himself of all outward signs of one true Godness and took the form of a servant instead (Philippians 2:6–7). The word *emptied* is hard to understand. It might help to think of a firefighter.

When firefighters are called on to fight a fire, they wear uniforms—special coats, helmets, and protective gloves and boots. They might wear oxygen masks to help them breathe if they need to enter a smoke-filled building. Thank God for brave men and women firefighters who protect us!

Now, when the firefighters go home at night and take off these special uniforms, do they stop being firefighters? Of course not. Firefighters are firefighters, whether they are wearing a firefighter coat and helmet or comfy pajamas! The way firefighters look on the outside doesn't change who they are on the inside.

When Jesus came down to live on earth, He "emptied himself" of all outside signs that He was God. It was as if He took them off and put them to the side. When Jesus was born on Christmas Day in Bethlehem, He took off His Godness and put on skin. He laid aside His crown.

He became human just like you and me. Suddenly, Jesus wasn't in all places at all times. He had come down from His perfect home in heaven to take care of His children. Because Jesus took off His Deity uniform (*deity* means God), did He stop being God? No! Jesus was fully God and fully man when He came down and lived on this earth. Jesus was the most fully alive human who has ever lived.

Maybe the three greatest words in the entire world are *God came down*. At Christmas, the One who had always existed became a newborn baby. The strongest person in the universe became a weak human. Robes of splendor were switched for strips of cloth. The One who owned all things became poor. The One who formed the stars lay beneath the stars. The One who created trees was laid into a manger made from trees. The One for whom the world cried now cried for His mother, Mary. The One who made life was born into a world of death. The artist who created light was born into a world of darkness. The One who came to save would soon be made to suffer. The baby in a wooden manger would redeem His people by being nailed to a wooden cross.

God came down. How magnificent! Jesus humbled Himself by coming down to us. Have more stunning and significant words ever been spoken? Jesus came down from a place of greatness, wonder, and splendor to a world of sin, darkness, and death. And He did it to love you. That's how special you are.

No matter what month it is, and no matter what day it is, *Merry Christmas!*

Dear Jesus, the One Who Came Down from Heaven,

Thank You for humbling Yourself and coming to earth. Thank You for taking off all the outward signs that showed You were God. You took on skin so that You could take on pain, suffering, and death and give me life.

Sometimes the noise and busyness of the world overwhelms the miracle of Christmas, which is when You came down. Even on the noisiest of days, please never stop whispering this truth to my heart.

I pray in the name of Jesus, the One Who Came Down from Heaven. Amen.

> Truly, truly, I say to you, whoever believes has eternal life. I am the bread of life. Your fathers ate the manna in the wilderness, and they died. This is the bread that comes down from heaven, so that one may eat of it and not die. I am the living bread that came down from heaven. If anyone eats of this bread, he will live forever.
> —John 6:47–51

Jesus is called...

The Prophet Who Has Come into the World—John 6:14

The Bread That Came Down from Heaven—John 6:41

The Living Bread That Came Down from Heaven—John 6:51

The One Who Came Down from Heaven—John 6:42

Jesus Is the Great Physician

Can you think of a time when you were sick? Sometimes in the middle of the night, you may call out to Mommy and Daddy when you feel bad. They may put their hands on your head and take your temperature. I'll bet sometimes you get to crawl into their bed too.

Getting sick is no fun. You have to stay inside and rest while your friends are outside playing. You might have to miss school and all the fun activities your teacher has planned. Sometimes you may be so sick that you don't even care about not being able to play with your friends.

Once in a while, you may be sick enough that you have to go see the doctor. Another word for doctor is *physician*. Physicians listen to you breathe, look in your ears, look at your throat, and press on your tummy. Sometimes they give you medicine or even a shot, all to help you feel better and help your body heal.

Sometimes when you are really sick, you may need to go to a hospital. I hope that doesn't happen to you! But if it does, doctors will be there to take care of you, and Jesus will be right there beside you.

Did you know that Jesus is the Great Physician? Although He is not directly called the Great Physician, followers of Jesus have referred to Him by this title for centuries. This is because He is the greatest doctor who ever lived! In the Bible, we can read stories of how He healed sick people by touching them. He could heal just by using His words too. He had the power to heal people from sickness, blindness, not being able to walk, and even death! He truly is the Great Physician.

But Jesus didn't come to earth to heal only our sick bodies. The main reason Jesus came was to heal our sick hearts. We all suffer from something worse than the sickness of our bodies. No medicine can fix our sick hearts, which are sick because of sin. We can't rest enough, take different medicines, or do enough healthy things to make our hearts clean and healthy again.

When we say we don't need Jesus to heal our sick hearts, Jesus says we are spiritually blind. We can still see with our eyes but be blind in our hearts. We need Jesus. He is the only One who can make sick hearts better again.

When we give our sick hearts to Jesus, He heals us and lets us live new lives! We will forever have healthy and forgiven hearts. And one day, Jesus will heal the hearts and bodies of all people who love Him, and they will go to heaven to live forever with Him. And do you know how many hospitals there are in heaven? Zero! There are no broken bones, no viruses, no cancer, no disease. In heaven, there aren't even Band-Aids because no one ever skins their knees! How amazing will that be?

The only way our hearts can be healed and we can be with Jesus in heaven is by trusting Him. We need to tell Him about our sick hearts and ask Him to forgive us. He knows our hearts are sick. That is why He came to earth to be with us. He showed us how much He wanted us to have healthy hearts when He died on the cross. Jesus loves us so much!

Dear Jesus, the Great Physician,

Thank You for being the healer of sick bodies and sick hearts.

I pray that You would heal my heart from selfishness. I ask that You heal my heart from anything that makes me think I should be the boss.

Every time I see a doctor, please remind me that You are the greatest doctor who ever lived. And one day, You will take me to heaven, where I will never need to go to the doctor's office again.

I pray in the name of Jesus, the Great Physician.

Amen.

> And when Jesus heard it, he said to them, "Those who are well have no need of a physician, but those who are sick. I came not to call the righteous, but sinners."
> —Mark 2:17

Jesus is called...

Physician—Mark 2:15–17

Jesus demonstrates the power to heal—Matthew 14:14, Mark 5:21–34

Jesus Is Master

It's fun to be the boss! When you are the boss, you get to make choices that can affect others.

Maybe you were the student of the day, so the teacher let you choose what game everyone would play at recess. Maybe your parents took you out for a special dinner, and you got to choose the restaurant. Maybe you have been asked to watch over a little brother or sister, so you were able to be the teacher when you played school.

When you are the boss, do you like to tell other people what to do? Do you make others do chores that maybe you should do? When you make decisions, do you choose things that will be fun for only you? Or do you understand the responsibility that comes with being the boss? When you are the boss, you need to be extra caring of others.

There are many different kinds of bosses. There are girl bosses and boy bosses. There are old bosses and young bosses. Maybe your Mommy and Daddy have a boss. I hope they have a boss who leads them well and wants them to do their very best.

Jesus said some important things about how bosses should treat other people. Jesus said that when we are the boss, we should care for people better than we care for ourselves! He said that bosses should be loving and forgiving, and the greatest bosses actually serve the people who work for them.

In the Bible, the disciples often called Jesus their *Master*, which is another word for boss. When they called Jesus *Master*, they were saying that Jesus is the One who had authority over their lives. Jesus being the Master meant that the disciples were servants.

The Bible has a very special word for servant. The word is *doulos*. You might need some help from your parents to pronounce this word. The word *doulos* is found throughout the New Testament, but the Gospel writer Luke liked to use it the most. Luke said that servants should be loyal and wise. They should know the will of the Master. That means that you know what the Master wants, and you do it. When the Bible calls us to live as servants, it is reminding us that Jesus is the Master.

Luke also said that no servant can have two masters (Luke 16:13). That just won't work. Some people live very sad lives because their master is money, and money is a terrible master. The only one who should be our master is Jesus!

When the Bible talks about Jesus being your Master, it is saying something amazing about Jesus. Even though He is the Master, He tells His followers that He did not come to earth to be served but to serve (Mark 10:45). Jesus is the Master, and yet He serves us! He came to pay the price to set us free from a life of sin and death. Before being crucified on a cross, Jesus washed the feet of His disciples. In those days, a master could not ask a slave to touch his feet. And yet, when Jesus washed their feet, He did what was never done, even by a slave.

Sometimes things just seem backward and upside down. Jesus is the Master, and yet He serves us. He is the Master, and He washed feet. He is the Master, and yet He is filled with compassion. There is no Master in the world like that.

Dear Jesus, my Master,

Thank You for being gracious, kind, and merciful. You are unlike any master the world has ever known. Thank You for being a serving Master.

Jesus, please help my heart to never want to serve more than one master. I pray that I will never make money my master. Please help me to serve only You!

Dear Master, please help me today to serve others. I pray that my heart would want to help people who are poor or suffering. Help me never be too proud to do things to help others.

I pray in the name of Jesus, my Master.
Amen.

> And a windstorm came down on the lake, and they were filling with water and were in danger. And they went and woke him, saying, "Master, Master, we are perishing!" And he awoke and rebuked the wind and the raging waves, and they ceased, and there was a calm. He said to them, "Where is your faith?" And they were afraid, and they marveled, saying to one another, "Who then is this, that he commands even winds and water, and they obey him?"
> —Luke 8:23–25

Jesus is called...

Master—Luke 5:5, Luke 17:13

Jesus Is the Good Shepherd

Have you ever had a cuddly stuffed lamb? Usually they have white fluffy fleece and are the perfect thing to snuggle up with at night.

What if you could have a real sheep as a pet? Would you like to snuggle up with a real sheep? Maybe so, but let's just say that a sheep might not be a very good pet. Sheep are pretty helpless and not very smart. Other animals are a lot smarter—you've probably seen all the things that animals like chimpanzees and dolphins and dogs can do! Even pigeons and pigs are considered pretty smart. But not sheep. You probably won't find them in a circus performing tricks.

Sheep need someone to take care of them. If a dog gets lost, he may be able to find the way home. But if a sheep is lost, he will never find his way home. And often there are animals lurking nearby that want to hurt the sheep. If a wolf attacks a flock of sheep, the sheep won't do anything to defend themselves! In fact, sheep often run into danger. If they come to the edge of a steep cliff, sheep will just keep on walking and go right over the edge! For so many reasons, sheep need a protector. They need a shepherd.

People who take care of sheep are called shepherds. And you might not know that sheep are actually good at one very special thing. In fact, of all the animals in the world, sheep might be the very best at this: Sheep know the voice of the shepherd. Your dog might come when he hears his owner's voice, and cats will *almost never* come when they hear their owner's voice. But a sheep will *almost always* come when it hears the voice of the shepherd.

Jesus tells us He is the Good Shepherd. He says His sheep hear His voice and follow Him. Like a shepherd, He calls His sheep by name. He shows them where to drink refreshing water and where to lie down to rest. If a sheep is lost, the Good Shepherd will look for as long as it takes to find the lost sheep and bring it home.

If Jesus is a Shepherd, what do His sheep look like? They look like us! We are His sheep. Jesus knows my name and your name. He calls to us. He cares for us. He protects us from the bad things that want to harm us. The Good Shepherd puts Himself in the way of the wolf and will give His life to protect His sheep. He keeps us from walking toward danger. And when we read the Bible, we can hear His voice and follow Him.

We know that Jesus gave up His life for His sheep and showed us how much He loves us when He was nailed to the cross and died. The good news of the Bible is that our Shepherd did not stay dead. He defeated the wolf of death and rose from the grave. He continues to call His sheep to Him. He wants to gather His flock around Him and tell us about His forever love. Jesus is the Good Shepherd.

Dear Jesus, the Good Shepherd,

Thank You for giving Your life for Your sheep.

I'm grateful You are a shepherd who guides, cares, and protects. Thank You that when I am lost, You look for me.

I confess to You that I am a sheep. I often want to go my own way and not make good decisions. Sometimes I do things that hurt the hearts of my friends as well as my own heart. Help me to listen to Your voice like sheep listen to the voice of their shepherd.

I pray in the name of my Jesus, my Shepherd.

Amen.

"I am the good shepherd. The good shepherd lays down his life for the sheep."
—John 10:11

Jesus is called...

The Shepherd of the Sheep—Matthew 9:36, John 10:2

The Good Shepherd—John 10:11–14

The Door of the Sheep—John 10:7

Jesus Is a Carpenter

Sometimes it's fun to think about what you will be when you grow up. You may even pretend you are a doctor, a veterinarian, a teacher, or a builder of tall buildings. Maybe you dream of being a professional ballerina, a police officer, a pastor, or a paleontologist! Maybe you hope that one day you could become a baker or an artist.

When you are asked what you want to be or do when you grow up, you might think about what your parents do and say you want to be just like them. If your mommy is a writer, you might want to write. If your daddy likes to build things, you might want to be a builder too.

When Jesus was growing up, boys often had the same jobs as their daddies. So, if your dad was a shepherd, you were likely a shepherd. If your dad made pots out of clay, you would learn from him how to make pots too. If your father was a fisherman, you likely caught your first fish when you were still a little boy.

Jesus' earthly dad, Joseph, was a carpenter. Some carpenters had the job of building houses. Others would build things that people would use around their house, like tables and chairs. Still other carpenters would build things for farmers, like plows, wheels, and a giant M-shaped object called a yoke that was used to train oxen.

We know Jesus was taught at a young age how to make things out of wood, like His father did. Think about this for a moment. Jesus likely learned how to make stools, chests, and other things to use in the home. Jesus probably knew how to make windows. He had to learn how to hammer and make wooden pieces fit together perfectly.

As He was building things next to His dad, Jesus probably heard many stories. He and Joseph likely had times of laughter, times to ask questions, times of hard work, and times to learn more about one another. It was probably a lot like the time you have with your parents.

Jesus had to watch closely to learn how to do His job—to choose a piece of wood and use the tools carefully. I'm sure He got better as He learned. Maybe His first chair was wobbly. Maybe His first table wasn't very straight. Joseph would have taught his son how to be a skilled carpenter.

It's interesting to think about what Jesus' life was like when most people still didn't know the important job He had been sent to earth to do. When He began preaching and teaching, those who knew Him as a boy remembered Him as being Mary and Joseph's son, a carpenter.

When Jesus went back to His hometown as a grown-up, people did not realize He was much more than a man and a carpenter. They would soon see that Jesus was God. Jesus would build more than tables and chairs. He was building His Church, and nothing in this world could ever destroy what He built.

Dear Jesus, the Carpenter,

Thank You for building more than tables and chairs. You are the Carpenter who builds new hearts and new lives. I'm thankful You built Your Church. And I'm thankful that nothing in the world is strong enough to destroy what You build.

Jesus, build in my heart a greater love for my family, my friends, and my neighbors. Make me a more faithful follower of You. Create a stronger love for You in the deepest places in my heart.

I pray in the name of Jesus, the Carpenter who builds new lives. Amen.

> And on the Sabbath he began to teach in the synagogue, and many who heard him were astonished, saying, "Where did this man get these things? What is the wisdom given to him? How are such mighty works done by his hands? Is not this the carpenter, the son of Mary and brother of James and Joses and Judas and Simon?"
> —Mark 6:1–3

Jesus is called...

Carpenter—Matthew 13:55, Mark 6:1–3

Jesus Is the Truth

Have you ever made up a pretend story to share? Maybe you told a story where you had superpowers. In your story you could fly! How amazing would that be? But let's say when you were telling your story about flying you said that your ten best friends were there, and they were flying too.

If I heard your story and wondered if it was true, how could I find out? Here is one hint: I could talk to your ten best friends and ask them if they really did see you flying around with superpowers. Unless you were actually Superman, I would probably find out that you were just making up a silly story for fun!

The Bible is full of stories, but unlike superhero stories, the Bible's stories are all 100 percent true. How do we know for sure? There are many, many answers to this question, but here are a few things to think about—and each of them has to do with a very important name of Jesus!

Jesus is Truth. Here is a fun way to think about this. Jesus is the Truth, and the Bible is the truth about the Truth! How can we know that the Bible is the truth?

If you were making up some of the stories in the Bible, you would write them a lot differently! For example, the Gospel of John says that three women were standing at the cross when Jesus was put to death. Can you name all three women? Read John 19:25. Their names were Mary, Mary, and Mary! If you were making up that story, would you give all three women the same name? Of course not! That would be silly!

Here is another way we can know the Bible is true: Jesus was a brother. That's right. Jesus was Mary's first baby, but He was not the only baby she had. The Bible tells us that Joseph and Mary had at least seven children. That's a big family! We know Jesus was the oldest child. We do not know all the names of Jesus' sisters, but we do know the names of Jesus' four brothers, James, Joses, Judas, and Simon.

If you were making up a story about Jesus, you wouldn't give the names of His brothers. If the stories about Jesus were just pretend, his brothers and sisters would know and could tell people the stories weren't true. But the stories were true. Every single detail of every single story in the Bible is the truth!

People did ask questions of Jesus' family. And Jesus' siblings knew that the brother they grew up with was very special. He lived a sinless life. His own family knew He was the Redeemer.

If you were making up stories about Jesus, you wouldn't say that He appeared to more than five hundred people after He defeated death by rising from the grave. That means five hundred people knew the truth! And many of them would still be alive when the story was written. You could find them, and they could tell you the stories were true. And that is just what people did.

In his Gospel, John said that Jesus is the Truth. Because Jesus is the Truth, we can trust everything He says, and we can have great confidence in the Bible. It is God's truth about the Truth!

Dear Jesus, the Truth,

Thank You that the Bible is true. Thank You for including so many stories that would only be in the Bible if they were true.

Help me to trust Your truth in all things. On days when I have doubts, help me to believe in my heart that everything in the Bible is true.

Please help me to be loving toward all my siblings, my cousins, and my friends. Just as Jesus was a patient and caring brother, help me to be helpful around my family.

I pray in the name of Jesus, the Truth!

Amen.

> Jesus said to him, "I am the way, and the truth, and the life. No one comes to the Father except through me."
> —John 14:6

Jesus is called...

The Truth—John 1:5, John 12:35–36

The Man Who Told You the Truth

He Heard from God—John 8:40

Jesus Is the Bridegroom

Weddings are a big deal. There are usually lots of beautiful flowers and pretty music. Everyone dresses up in nice clothes. Perhaps you have been to a wedding. Maybe you have even been *in* a wedding as a flower girl or a ringbearer. As the people in the wedding get ready, there is always a lot of excitement. Whether you're in a church or outside, when you are there, you can tell that it is a special day.

One day Jesus was teaching the disciples when He said, "And if I go and prepare a place for you, I will come again and will take you to myself, that where I am you may be also" (John 14:3). When the disciples heard this, they knew Jesus was saying He is the Bridegroom. Let me explain. . . .

In the days of Jesus, when a man fell in love with a woman, they would promise one another that they would one day be married. They would have a special engagement ceremony. After that ceremony, for the whole next year, the man and woman would remain apart. The bride-to-be (the woman) would not see the bridegroom-to-be (the man) until the wedding day.

During that year, the bride would get ready for the day her bridegroom would come back. And while she waited, she knew what the bridegroom was doing. He was spending the entire year building a house right next door to the house where he grew up. This is the house where the new couple would live together when they were officially married.

After one year, the new house would be finished. And on a night that would be a surprise to the bride, the groom would call his friends together, and they would walk to the bride's house, each one carrying a torch. And when they were close to the house of the bride, the friends of the bridegroom would begin to yell as loud as they could, "The bridegroom is coming!"

Can you imagine how excited the bride would be when she heard that shout! She had been dreaming about this moment for a year! She would quickly call her friends together, and then the bride and groom and their friends would walk together to the new home. And there they had the biggest party you can imagine! The new home is where the marriage ceremony would happen. In the time Jesus lived on earth, the wedding celebration would last for several days!

When people heard Jesus say that He was going away to prepare a place for them, they understood what He was saying. He would leave this earth. But one day, Jesus the Bridegroom would return to take His bride to a place He had prepared where they could live forever. So you might be wondering… who is Jesus' bride? It's the Church! Those who love Jesus are part of God's family, His church. That's you and me!

Jesus gave us a wonderful promise. Right now, today, at this exact moment, Jesus is preparing a place for His children. And one day, there will be a shout! The Bridegroom will return, and He will take us home to heaven to be with Him forever.

Jesus loves the Church. The Bible uses the idea of a bridegroom standing at the wedding, waiting for His beautiful bride to give us an idea of the great love Jesus has for us. He loves the bride and promises to love, protect, and care for her. This is how Jesus feels about you.

Dear Jesus, the Bridegroom,

Thank You for promising that You are preparing a place where I will one day go to live with You forever.

Help me to live my life preparing for Your return. I want to be ready when one day You come back to take Your bride, Your people, home to heaven.

I pray in the name of Jesus, the Bridegroom. Amen.

And Jesus said to them, "Can the wedding guests mourn as long as the bridegroom is with them? The days will come when the bridegroom is taken away from them, and then they will fast."
—Matthew 9:15

Jesus is called...

The Bridegroom—Mark 2:19–20, John 3:29

Jesus Is the True Vine

Does your family like to visit a pumpkin patch in the fall? It's fun to explore and look for the fattest or tallest pumpkin. As you walk through the patch, you have to be careful. All over the ground, strong, thick vines are attached to the pumpkins. Along the vines you'll find smaller branches with bright yellowish-orange flowers. If you come back to the pumpkin patch next year, those flowers will have turned into the beautiful fruit of a pumpkin.

The pumpkins are growing because of the work of a pumpkin farmer. He plants the vines and closely watches them grow. He may need to cut off or prune some bad branches that look sick. Those branches will not grow healthy fruit.

Learning about how pumpkins grow can help us understand why Jesus calls Himself the Vine. He says we are the branches and God is the vinedresser (what we might call the farmer). When you trust Jesus, you are a part of Him, much like the branch is attached to the vine. And you are being loved, nourished, and cared for in three very important ways.

First, by being attached to the vine, the branch is taking in everything the vine has to give. Jesus taught His disciples that the vine gives love and life to the branch. When you stay attached to the Vine (Jesus), you will be given great joy and everything you need to have a full heart and life. Good things will begin to happen because healthy branches grow healthy fruit.

But the fruit you will grow is much different than pumpkins! You will grow a desire to tell others about Jesus. You will want to do things to honor Jesus out of love for Him.

You will want to find ways to serve in your church, neighborhood, and school. You won't need to do any of these things to make Jesus love you more. You will do these things because He loves you. Nothing eternally good will happen in your life unless you are attached to Jesus, the Vine.

Second, the vine is being loved and cared for when the farmer cuts back the branches. Sometimes you make sinful choices that do not honor God. When this happens, you need to ask Him for forgiveness and stop filling your heart and life with sin. This is like the farmer pruning the bad parts of the branches. Pruning may not feel good, but the result is beautiful, healthy fruit. Why would God prune a branch that is growing fruit? So that it will grow more fruit! Pruning is always for your good and for God's glory.

Third, branches are attached to other branches through the vine. God created you to live in a community with other friends who are also attached to the Vine. God is the greatest farmer ever, and He knows you need friends to encourage you, pray for you, and love you. You can be connected to these God-loving friends through the Vine, Jesus.

Keep your branch connected to Jesus and watch your fruit grow—love, joy, peace, patience, kindness, goodness, faith, gentleness, and self-control. What a harvest!

Dear Jesus, the True Vine,

I have life only because of You. Thank You for giving me all I need.

Jesus, You said that apart from You, I can do nothing. Please help me to believe that the truly meaningful things I will do in this life will only happen because I am attached to You.

I confess that sometimes I do things that are wrong. Give me patience when God is pruning me. Help me to remember it is because He loves me.

Help me find Christian friends who will help me know and serve You. I pray in the name of Jesus, the Vine and the source of my life. Amen.

> "I am the true vine, and my Father is the vinedresser. Every branch in me that does not bear fruit he takes away, and every branch that does bear fruit he prunes, that it may bear more fruit."
> —John 15:1–2

Jesus is called...

The True Vine—John 15:1

The Vine—John 15:4

Jesus of Nazareth

Have you ever gotten lost? Being lost is very scary. Maybe you were in a big crowd of people, and you got separated from your mommy or daddy. Or maybe you were old enough to walk home from school, but on the way, you took a wrong turn and were suddenly lost.

One of the first things we learn in school is our address. It is important to be able to tell people where we live. If a neighbor or a police officer stopped to help you, they would want to know where you live.

First, we might learn what street we live on and what city we live in. Then we learn what state we live in. We finally learn what country we live in. That way, no matter where you are in the world, you can always find your way home.

The place you live is called a community, and it's important. The friends we play with are there. Our cousins and grandparents may live nearby. We may go to school and church in our neighborhood. Our community is filled with people who know us and care about us.

Jesus grew up in a community too. He lived in more than one place, so He knows what it feels like to move. He was born in Bethlehem, but He did not grow up there. He grew up in a small village called Nazareth with his mother, father, brothers, and sisters. Nazareth was in a region called Galilee in the country of Israel. It was fifteen miles from the Sea of Galilee and twenty miles from the Mediterranean Sea. The village was so tiny that people thought nothing important could ever happen in Nazareth.

The people in Nazareth had known Jesus as a little boy who played and lived among them. They watched Him grow and play with their own children. They knew the names of all his brothers and sisters. Jesus watched His earthly father, who was a carpenter, and eventually learned from His dad how to be a carpenter Himself. Maybe He made things for the neighbors in Nazareth. Jesus would have studied God's Word with the men there and attended the temple to worship God.

But one day it was time for Jesus to leave the community and begin to teach others about God's message of love and forgiveness for all. He had to leave His home in Nazareth and say goodbye to His friends and family. He walked to the places God would lead Him. There He would tell the people the Good News about God's plan to rescue them from their sins.

After Jesus left Nazareth, He would never have a home of His own. He would sleep outside or be invited to stay with a friend. Jesus was

from Nazareth, but He knew that His real home is heaven, where He lives now with His heavenly Father. That is Jesus' real, forever address.

If you love Jesus, your forever address is with Jesus in heaven. That will be an easy address to remember! You will be a part of a community that will forever love you.

Dear Jesus of Nazareth,

Thank You that one day I will go to my forever home in heaven, where I will live with You forever and ever.

Thank You for my hometown. Thank You for the community where I now live. I ask You to help me be a good friend to all those in my community. Please bless my hometown with strong churches, strong leaders, and people who deeply care for one another.

I pray in the name of Jesus of Nazareth.
Amen.

> Philip found Nathanael and said to him, "We have found him of whom Moses in the Law and also the prophets wrote, Jesus of Nazareth, the son of Joseph." Nathanael said to him, "Can anything good come out of Nazareth?" Philip said to him, "Come and see."
> —John 1:45–46

Jesus is called...

Jesus the Nazarene—Mark 14:67

Jesus of Nazareth—Luke 4:34, Luke 24:19

Jesus the Galilean—Matthew 26:69

Jesus Is the Hope of Israel

People are chosen to do things for a lot of really strange and silly reasons. Sometimes people get to do special things just because they are boys. Other times, the tallest person in the room gets to be the boss. Occasionally, the strongest person gets to be the leader. If you have brothers and sisters, you know that Mom and Dad might ask the oldest to be in charge. Maybe you have watched the smartest person in class get chosen to do something important. Sometimes grownups pick the person with the most money to be the boss.

People have been selected in unfair ways since Bible times. When the Old Testament was written, an oldest son was the boss of all the other children, even if he had older sisters. Leaders were often chosen by people because they were the strongest, oldest, and tallest. They were selected because they came from the most powerful family. In 1 Samuel 9 and 10, the people chose Saul to be their king because he was the tallest and the strongest. And you know what? He ended up being a not-so-good king.

But the Bible is full of wonderful stories of God making choices that seemed to be the opposite of what people said should be done. The people said that only strong people can get the job done, so God chose a man named Gideon, who was the weakest member of the weakest family, to do something really important. Esau was older, stronger, and more skilled, but God chose his brother, Jacob.

People said only boys could lead an army, but God chose Deborah to lead Israel into battle and on to victory. Aaron was the oldest and a much better speaker, but God chose Moses to lead the Israelites out of Egypt. David was the youngest of all his brothers, but he was chosen by God to defeat a giant and become a king. Rachel was the prettiest, but God chose her sister, Leah, to be a grandmother of Jesus. Judah was the fourth-born son and had a very messy heart, but God chose him to be one of Jesus' grandfathers.

Over and over again, when the people thought they knew how someone should be chosen, God did something very different. Israel was a small, weak nation full of people who often turned away from God. And yet God chose them to be His special people. He had a plan for them, and all of God's unlikely choices were part of that plan. They led to God sending His Son, Jesus, to save Israel. Jesus came to earth to be the Hope and King of Israel.

In the Old Testament book of Deuteronomy, God tells us why He chose Israel. In chapter 7, God tells His chosen people that it was not because they were bigger and more powerful than other nations. Can you guess why? God loved and chose Israel . . . just because! How wonderful is that?

Your parents love you, and they would choose you over and over again! Is it because you are big and strong? Is it because you are smart or pretty? Do they love you because you do all your chores? Nope. They love you just because they do. That is why God loved Israel, and that's why God loves you. The Israelites were chosen by God. And if you love Jesus, you are God's chosen too!

Our heavenly Father sent Jesus to be the Hope of Israel, and He is your hope too.

Dear Jesus, the Hope of Israel,

I'm grateful You came to earth to save Your chosen people. Thank You for choosing people to do Your work even though they were not always the tallest, the oldest, the prettiest, or the strongest. You choose the weak of this world to do the most important things in this world.

Jesus, You have created everyone to be special. Please help me to never overlook anyone because of the way they look. Help me to see people with the eyes of God.

I pray in the name of Jesus, the One who chose me!
Amen.

They took branches of palm trees and went out to meet him, crying out, "Hosanna! Blessed is he who comes in the name of the Lord, even the King of Israel!"
—John 12:13

Jesus is called...

God of Israel—Matthew 15:31

King of Israel—Matthew 27:42

The One to Redeem Israel—Luke 24:21

29
Jesus Is the Savior of the World

Have you ever had an awful, completely horrible kind of day? The kind of day where nothing goes right? Maybe you couldn't find your socks, you forgot to bring your umbrella to the bus stop, you got into trouble in class without meaning to, and your best friend sat with someone else at lunch. That kind of day.

Days like that sometimes leave us feeling sad. Maybe we want to give up on trying to be really good at soccer. Maybe we want to quit a dance class because we feel out of place. Maybe we want to walk away from piano lessons because we can't make our fingers move the right way. We start to feel sad, and we lose hope that we will ever be any good at anything, have the right friends, or fit in.

In those not-so-good moments, we might find ourselves wishing for someone to step in and save the day. To make things better by showing us exactly how to make that play, finish that song, or meet that new friend. To encourage us not to give up and remind us that tomorrow we can hope for a better day.

Before Jesus was born, the people who lived in the nation of Israel were having lots of not-so-good days too.

They wanted to be free, but they were living under the rule of unkind leaders. The people were hoping for a savior to deliver them. A savior is someone who rescues others. A savior helps people by guarding, protecting, and saving. In the first chapter of Matthew, God tells Joseph that Mary is going to have a baby who will grow up to save people from their sins. God also said that Joseph was to name the baby Jesus, which means, "God saves." God made it very clear that the Savior the people had been waiting for was Jesus!

So take a deep breath, my friends. We will have tough days when we want to give up on something because we are frustrated or sad.

Everyone has times when it feels like nothing is going right. And when that happens, you might have some great friends, coaches, or teachers who can help and encourage you. But humans can't always save the day, and they definitely can't save us from our sins. Always remember that you have a Savior who is guarding and protecting you—Jesus! He will never, ever let you down, and He will give you that deep-in-your-heart hope that will last forever.

Did you hear that great news? Jesus is the Living Hope for everyone. He might not show you exactly how to kick a soccer ball, but He will never give up on you. He will always and forever love you, pursue you, care for you, and fill your heart with hope. He is so much more than the one who saves the day; Jesus is the Savior of the world!

Dear Jesus, the Savior of the World,

I know that because you are the Savior, you are the Hope of everyone, everywhere. You shine light into the darkness. You bring love when people hate. Thank You for bringing good to a world that is too often harmed by bad. Thank You for dying on the cross so I could know love and life.

Please help me to always remember that You are the Savior. Even on the worst day of my whole life, when it feels like everything is against me, show me there is hope because there is You. Even on the darkest night, please allow me to see Your light.

I know some people don't believe You are the Savior of the World. Help them today to see that You are the one they have been looking for to bring them hope.

I pray in the name of Jesus, my Hope and my Savior.

Amen.

> And many more believed because of his word. They said to the woman, "It is no longer because of what you said that we believe, for we have heard for ourselves, and we know that this this is indeed the Savior of the world."
> —John 4:41–42

Jesus is called...

Savior—Luke 2:11

Savior of the World—John 4:42

Jesus Is the Cornerstone

I'm sure you have a lot of experience building things with blocks. Whether you choose wooden blocks or plastic blocks, building with them is wonderful fun. It's exciting to have a contest with a friend to see who can make the biggest building. Maybe you have made a building taller than the top of your head!

But sometimes the building gets really wobbly and falls over. Have you ever thought about what could make your building strong and sturdy so that you can build it higher? It's all about the foundation. The *foundation* is the base or the lowest level of your building. It's very important. In fact, it's the most important part of any building.

Professional builders who build really big buildings call the first corner they put in place the *cornerstone*. Everything else in the building is measured off this first stone. If the cornerstone is crooked, the whole building will be crooked. If the cornerstone is perfectly straight, then the whole building will be straight. It is really, *really* important to get the cornerstone right!

In chapter 21 of his gospel, Matthew tells a story about a day when Jesus was teaching a large crowd. Jesus reminded the people of Psalm 118. It says the cornerstone will be rejected, but it is marvelous in the Lord's eyes. To be rejected means people turn away from you. They don't want to have anything to do with you.

This Bible verse might seem confusing at first. Why would anyone reject a perfectly good cornerstone? And how could being rejected be marvelous? Didn't the builders want the building to be strong and perfect? Well, the cornerstone being talked about here isn't an actual piece of building material; it's Jesus!

Psalm 118 says that Jesus is our Cornerstone, the first piece that makes everything straight and strong. When it says the Cornerstone was rejected, it was talking about how the people who lived at the same time as Jesus rejected Him as their Cornerstone. They thought they could build their lives on other cornerstones, like money, power, and being liked by lots of people. But those things are not good cornerstones.

Your life will be filled with many good things. You might go to college. One day you might get married and have children of your own. One day you will have a job. But the most important thing by far is to build your life on the right cornerstone. If you don't, everything else in life will be crooked. If Jesus is not the Cornerstone of your heart, your life will not be strong enough to go through the many happy and sad times that lie ahead. Jesus is the marvelous Cornerstone who can save us from our sins.

The next time you build a tower with blocks, pay attention to that very first block, the cornerstone. And as you build a strong and tall building, remember that Jesus needs to be the Cornerstone of your heart. He is the most important thing in your life! His foundation is a marvelous and precious gift from God to you.

Dear Jesus, the Cornerstone,

I want to build my entire life on You! You are the one I'll use to measure all of life.

Jesus, other people will try to tell me they will be a better cornerstone than You. Some people will tell me money is the best cornerstone. Other people will tell me that the way I look is the best cornerstone. But I want to remember always that You—and nothing else—are the perfect Cornerstone. Help me live a strong and sturdy life because I have built it on You.

I pray in the name of Jesus, my Cornerstone.
Amen.

> "Have you not read this Scripture: 'The stone that the builders rejected has become the cornerstone; this was the Lord's doing, and it is marvelous in our eyes'?"
> —Mark 12:10–11

Jesus is called...

Cornerstone—Matthew 21:42, Luke 20:17

The Stone the Builders Rejected—Matthew 21:42

Jesus Is the Door

Doors can be pretty amazing if you think about them. When a door opens, you can walk through and instantly find yourself in a different place. Sometimes you can go from darkness into light. Other times you can go from fear to safety.

And there are so many types of doors—front doors, back doors, sliding doors, car doors, elevator doors, and revolving doors. There are wooden doors, metal doors, glass doors, and even doggie doors. There are big doors and little doors. And there are human doors! That's right! Sometimes people can be doors! Does that sound silly?

People who take care of sheep are called shepherds. In Bible times, when the weather was nice, the shepherd would stay with his flock of sheep in the rolling hills where there was lots of delicious green grass for the sheep to eat. And at night, do you think the shepherd would leave the sheep? Do you think the shepherd would stay in a hotel? No! The shepherd never left his sheep. At night, the shepherd would sleep with his sheep.

Because the sheep would eat a lot of grass, and the shepherd was always in search of the best grass, the sheep would move from hillside to hillside. Over several months, they might never spend the night in the same place twice! Each night, the shepherd would build a new pen for the sheep. He would look around and find some big rocks. Then he would build a big circle out of the rocks, leaving one gap in the circle.

He would place some thorn bush branches on top of the rocks too. If he had been building a pen for horses or cows, the gap is where he would put a gate. But the sheep pen didn't have a gate. Instead, the gap is where the shepherd would sleep. He would become the door!

When Jesus tells us He is the Door, He is reminding us that He is the Good Shepherd who gives up His life for His sheep. He is telling us He is guarding, protecting, caring, watching, and loving His flock. After all, a shepherd never stopped working. Even while the shepherd slept, he was still guarding his sheep. Jesus is watching over you, every second of every day. Even while you sleep!

Because God loved us so much, He sent a Door. He sent Jesus. The only way the door opens is if we give our broken, sinful hearts to the only One who can save us from our sins.

Others will try to tell us they are the door, but the Bible says they are thieves and robbers. Only Jesus is the true Door that we may enter by giving our messy, broken, and sad hearts to Him. He is the only One who can fix our broken hearts. He is the Good Shepherd who lays His life down to protect His flock, all those under His care. Jesus is the Door.

Dear Jesus, the Door,

Thank You for giving Your life for Your sheep and for being the Shepherd who guides, cares, and protects.

When people say they are the door to life, help me to remember that only You are the Door to life! Help my heart to know that only You will always speak words of truth and life. Help me to know when thieves and robbers are trying to trick me into believing things that are not true. Jesus, I want to live under Your watch and in Your care.

I pray in the name of my Jesus, the Door of Life.
Amen.

> So Jesus again said to them, "Truly, truly, I say to you, I am the door of the sheep. All who came before me are thieves and robbers, but the sheep did not listen to them. I am the door. If anyone enters by me, he will be saved and will go in and out and find pasture. The thief comes only to steal and kill and destroy. I came that they may have life and have it abundantly."
> —John 10:7–10

Jesus is called...

The Door—John 10:1

The Door of the Sheep—John 10:7

Jesus Is the Stairway to Heaven

Have you ever thought about how important stairways are? We use them all the time, up and down, down and up. But we also take them for granted. What if you lived in a two-story house but there was no stairway to the upstairs? Or what if you lived at the top of an apartment building and there weren't any stairs to get there? How would you get to your room at night? Stairways are necessary and helpful when we want to go places.

Some stairs are covered in soft carpet. Maybe that's the kind Grandma has at her house. Those are the kind that are fun to slide down. Some are very curvy and called spirals. We have to be careful when going up and down those. We don't want to fall down! Have you ever been to a big sports stadium and, just for fun, walked to the very top? That is a lot of stairs! Some stairs are very steep. When we get to the top, we have to catch our breath.

When you walk up a set of stairs, you are *ascending* the stairs. When you slide down, walk down, or hop down stairs, you are *descending* the stairs. Those seem like big words—*ascending* and *descending*—but they just mean going up and down.

Stairs have been around a long, long time. Way back in the Old Testament, Jacob had a dream about a huge stairway reaching all the way from the earth to heaven, and angels were going up and down the stairs (Genesis 28:12). Jacob woke up and knew that God was in that place!

Much later in the New Testament, Jesus tells about a similar scene and says that one day heaven will be opened and the angels of God will be seen going up and down, ascending and descending. But instead of using the word *stairway*, He says the angels are traveling on the *Son of Man*! (Remember, *Son of Man* is one of Jesus' names.) Wait... where are the angels going, and what does it mean they are walking on Jesus?

Jesus is being used as a staircase. Just like stairs connect different floors in a building, Jesus is the Stairway who connects heaven and earth. He is the only way to get to heaven—He is the Way! Jesus clearly says He is the only staircase that leads to heaven. In the Gospel of John, Jesus says that no one can reach His heavenly Father apart from Him (14:6). When we trust in Jesus as our Savior, we know we will one day live with God in heaven in His forever home.

Some people say that following rules is the stairway to heaven. Others say that being a good person and doing good things for others is the stairway to heaven. Although following rules and being kind to others are wonderful things, the only true way to heaven is believing Jesus is the stairs. Jesus Christ our Savior is the only Way, the only Truth, and the only Life.

Dear Jesus, the Stairway to Heaven,

I know many people will tell me there are many things I must do to climb the stairway to heaven. People will say the only way to climb the stairs is by giving away all my stuff. Others will say I need to be extra nice to my friends. Some will say to always obey my parents. I know that all throughout my life, people will give me a list of things I need to do for God to love me.

Jesus, help me always to remember that You don't give me a list because You are the list! It isn't a list of things I have to do that will get me to heaven, it's You! You are the stairs. The only thing I need to get to heaven is to follow You.

I still want to be a person who shares and is kind to everyone. And I want to obey my parents. But please help me to remember that these things will not take me to heaven. That is something only You can do!

I pray in the name of Jesus, the Stairway to Heaven.
Amen.

And he said to him, "Truly, truly, I say to you, you will see heaven opened, and the angels of God ascending and descending on the Son of Man."
—John 1:51

Jesus is called...

The Stairway to Heaven—John 1:51 (Genesis 28:12–13)

The Way, the Truth, and the Life—John 14:6

Jesus Is the One

"We're number one! We're number one!" Have you ever heard that chanted after a team wins a big game? People who support the winning team like to tell everyone their team is the best. Sometimes people buy a big giant *"We're number one!"* foam finger to wave in the air.

Maybe your mommy and daddy's favorite sports team has been struggling for a long time. And maybe a really good player just joined the team. You might hear your parents say the new player is the one who is going to turn everything around. Sometimes we say a certain leader is the one who is going to change the country. You might hear that a new pastor is the one who is going to bring hope to your church.

Did you know that Jesus is *"the One"*? But when we say that Jesus is the One, we mean something very different

than when we are talking about a sports star or a political leader or a new boss at work.

Jesus is the One chosen by God to preach the Good News to the poor. Jesus is the One who has been sent to bring freedom to the prisoners. Jesus is the One sent to tell everyone about God doing incredible things for people that they could never, ever do for themselves. Jesus is the One who fulfills the prophecies in the Bible.

Jesus is called the One who came not to be served, but to serve. There has never been anyone who serves as lovingly and as beautifully as Jesus. He came to serve you and me.

Jesus is called the One sent by God to redeem Israel. The people of Israel were a big mess. They had messy, sad hearts, just like us. They needed someone to save them by paying the price for their sins. Jesus is the only One who could do that by His death on the cross. And Jesus is the only One who conquered death and rose from the grave. He was the perfect sacrifice because He was the only One who lived a sinless life.

John the Baptist said Jesus is the One who baptizes with the Holy Spirit (John 1:33). When John the Baptist baptized Jesus, he saw heaven open, and the Spirit of God, in the form of a dove, came down and rested on Jesus. John knew Jesus was the One for whom a lost and dying world had been waiting.

Jesus is the One. He is the one and only Son of God. Jesus is the only One who could be the perfect sacrifice for our sins.

Imagine God sitting on the very top of a huge mountain. There is only one path up the mountain, and that path is Jesus. There is no other path. Jesus told His disciples He is the *only* Way, the *only* Truth, and the *only* Life (John 14:6). He told His disciples He is the One. The only way to God the Father is through Jesus. There is no one like Jesus. Be sure to follow Jesus, the One.

Dear Jesus, the One,

Thank You for being the only One who could be the bridge between heaven and earth. You are the only One who can connect people to God.

Please help me to remember that You are the only way to real life. People will tell me that money is the way to true happiness. Others will tell me that following my heart is the way to real joy. Some might even tell me that the only way to enjoy life is to be the boss of my own life. Jesus, I know that only You are the Way, the Truth, and the Life. No one has ever known God without You, Lord Jesus.

I pray in the name of Jesus, the Holy One of God.

Amen.

> As he was saying these things, a cloud came and overshadowed them, and they were afraid as they entered the cloud. And a voice came out of the cloud, saying, "This is my Son, my Chosen One; listen to him!"
> —Luke 9:34–35

Jesus is called...

The Holy One of God—Mark 1:24, John 6:69

The One Who Serves—Luke 22:27

The One to Redeem Israel—Luke 24:21

The One Who Baptizes with the Holy Spirit
—John 1:33

34
Jesus Is Called Sir (the One to Whom Respect Is Due)

Have you ever been to a wedding and wondered why everyone stood up when the bride began to walk down the aisle? It's one of the most special moments of the wedding! Everyone stands up as a sign of respect for the bride. Similarly, when a judge enters a courtroom, someone says, "All rise." Everyone in the room is expected to stand up to show respect to the judge.

Another way to show respect is by bowing down. If you ever have the chance to meet a king or queen, you will be expected to bow.

Can you think of other ways we show respect to people who help and care for us? God wants us to respect and obey many people because He has given them authority in our lives, people like our parents, teachers, pastors, police officers, and leaders of our country. Respect means we listen to them and pray for them. Even when we disagree with our leaders, we still respect them because of their authority.

Because all people are sinful, sometimes people who are in charge make mistakes.

Sometimes they make choices that are not the best. Teachers make mistakes and need to ask their students for forgiveness. Pastors make mistakes, and when they do, they should confess their mistake to God and ask forgiveness from those they hurt. But we still love and respect people who make mistakes.

Jesus is the most perfect leader who ever lived! He never sinned. If people who are sinful are worthy of our respect, how much more respect is Jesus worthy of? Jesus is worthy of both our praise and our respect.

When Jesus taught on this earth, many leaders were jealous of Him. They didn't like that people were following Jesus. But one day one of these important leaders came to Jesus and called Him "Sir" (John 4:49).

He respected Jesus. John's gospel tells us the man had a sick child and knew Jesus could do a miracle and heal his son. And that is just what Jesus did!

When the man called Jesus "Sir," he was saying Jesus is the One to whom respect is due. On another occasion, Mark tells the story of a leader who came to Jesus because his twelve-year-old girl was sick (Mark 5:22–23). Even though he was one of the religious leaders, he fell down before Jesus and worshipped him. He respected Jesus. He was hoping Jesus could heal his sick daughter. Amazingly, Jesus did more than heal his sick daughter. Jesus raised her from the dead!

All throughout Scripture, Jesus is addressed as "Sir," "Rabbi," "Rabonni," "Teacher," and "Good Teacher." These are all names of deep respect. Some of them are names we use when addressing the important people in our life.

Jesus deserves your respect. He will never make a mistake or do anything to hurt you. His decisions will always be the right ones. He loves you. He carried your sins to the cross and died the death you deserve.

The name of Jesus deserves the highest respect. We should always be very careful to only use His name in a manner that brings Him glory and honor. One day, at the very mention of the name of Jesus, everyone will show Jesus the greatest respect by bowing before Him (Philippians 2:10).

Who do you think is the most powerful person in the world? Whoever that person is, one day he or she will bow before Jesus with respect and confess that He is Lord. What a glorious day that will be!

Dear Jesus, Sir,

Thank You for being the One worthy of all my respect. Thank You for being a teacher without fault and a savior without sin.

Please help me to always use Your name in the right way, never in a disrespectful way when I am angry or frustrated. Every time I speak any of Your names, help me, Lord Jesus, to say it in a way that shows respect.

I respectfully pray in the name of Jesus.

Amen.

> When this man heard that Jesus had come from Judea to Galilee, he went to him and asked him to come down and heal his son, for he was at the point of death. So Jesus said to him, "Unless you see signs and wonders you will not believe." The official said to him, "Sir, come down before my child dies." Jesus said to him, "Go; your son will live." The man believed the word that Jesus spoke to him and went on his way.
> —John 4:46–50

Jesus is called...

Sir—John 5:7   **Rabbi**—John 11:8

Rabboni—John 20:16   **Teacher**—Matthew 8:19

Good Teacher—Mark 10:17

Jesus Is a Big Brother

Maybe you have brothers and sisters. And maybe you have a big brother. I have a big brother I sure do love. He is a very gifted artist and makes so many beautiful things. I love when he spends time with me and we get to make things together. He is a wonderful big brother.

When I was a little girl and some bullies in the neighborhood knocked me off my bike, I ran home in tears. My big brother was very worried when he saw me crying. He asked what had happened. When I told him about the bullies, he ran out the door. I was sure my big brother was going to protect me and take care of those bullies. When he got home later, I asked him what happened. He told me that he talked to them and then they played a game of baseball. I'm not exactly sure what happened, but those bullies never bothered me again.

A good big brother loves you and protects you from things that can hurt you. Because they are older, they are usually bigger and stronger. And sometimes, they are wiser.

The Bible calls Jesus a big Brother. Jesus had four brothers and at least two sisters. He was the oldest. We do not know all the names of Jesus' sisters, but the names of Jesus' brothers were James, Joses, Judas, and Simon. That means there were seven children in Jesus' home. I bet that was a noisy household! Jesus probably had to help His parents with lots of chores. Maybe when His mother and father were busy, they asked Jesus to watch His brothers and sisters. He probably taught His younger brothers and sisters lots of games. He might have shared a bed with a few of His brothers.

Did you know that the Bible tells us that Jesus is your big Brother? It's true! Paul was one of the apostles God used to spread His message around the world. In Romans 8, Paul writes that you have been chosen to be made into the image of Jesus, who is the firstborn of many brothers. That means when you choose to follow Jesus, He is your big Brother!

One time, Jesus was teaching a crowd of people when His mother and brothers told Him it was time for a family meeting. Jesus used that opportunity to teach us something very important about family: His family was not just His mother and brothers. His family is anyone who loves Him and does the will of the heavenly Father (Mark 3:34). Jesus wasn't saying anything bad about His mother and His brothers. He was saying that anyone can be a part of the family of God simply by following and obeying Jesus and His Father.

If you have brothers, they may not always be kind. You may argue and fight with them. There may be days when they don't want to play with you. And there might be days when they don't protect you. If you are a big brother, I hope you are always nice to your little brother or sister.

Jesus is the perfect big Brother. He is the One who loves you, teaches you, and defends you. You can always talk to Him. He will never leave you. Did you know that Jesus is different from any other big brother in the entire world? He did something only He could do. When He spread His arms out and willingly gave up His life on the cross, He was the only Brother who paid for your sins. He died the death you deserve so that you can live the life only He deserved.

Jesus is the best Big Brother ever!

Dear Jesus, my Big Brother,

Thank You for being my Big Brother.

Jesus, I want to obey You. Help me to follow You every day. I know that just obeying You will not make me a part of the family of God. Loving You because you first loved me—that is what makes me a part of the family of God. That is what makes You my Big Brother. Thank You for always caring for me, protecting me, and loving me, even when I can't see it or feel it. You are always there.

I pray in the name of Jesus, the greatest Big Brother ever! Amen.

> Someone told him, "Your mother and brothers are standing outside, wanting to speak to you." He replied to him, "Who is my mother, and who are my brothers?" Pointing to his disciples, he said, "Here are my mother and my brothers. For whoever does the will of my Father in heaven is my brother and sister and mother."
> —Matthew 12:47–50 NIV

Jesus is called...

Our Brother—John 20:17
(we share the same heavenly Father)

Brother of James, Joses, Judas, and Simon
—Mark 6:3

Jesus Is the Lamb of God

The Bible is filled with stories of people who have special titles. David was a king. Daniel was a prophet. Moses was a lawgiver, and Joshua was a general. Did you know that Abraham had no title? He was a man of faith who loved to pray. And that was enough!

One morning Abraham woke up bright and early. He probably couldn't sleep. The day before, an angel had appeared to him and told him to take his son Isaac to a nearby mountain and sacrifice him as an offering to the Lord. That's certainly not what anyone wants to hear from an angel. Isaac was Abraham's son, and Abraham loved him—a lot!

Abraham and his wife, Sarah, had prayed long and hard for a child. The Lord had finally answered their prayer with a beautiful son they named Isaac. And now, when Isaac was still a young man, God told Abraham to sacrifice him as a burnt offering. That means that God asked Abraham to kill his son! Amazingly, Abraham woke up early because he wanted to obey the Lord.

Abraham led Isaac on a three-day hike to the mountain God had chosen as the place where Isaac would be sacrificed. On the way, Isaac noticed something was missing. He saw that his father had the wood for an offering. He had the supplies to start a fire and a knife to kill the lamb. But Isaac pointed out that his father had forgotten to bring the lamb to be offered!

Abraham answered with some of the most important words that have ever been spoken. His words would be felt for centuries to come.

Abraham said, "God Himself will provide a lamb." When Abraham and Isaac got to the mountain, that is just what God did. He provided a lamb for Abraham to sacrifice in place of Isaac.

The theme of the Old Testament is a question—*Where is the Lamb?*—and an answer—*God will provide a Lamb.*

Over and over, the people of God asked Him for a savior. *God, we are oppressed, discouraged, and hopeless. Where is the Lamb?* And God would remind them over and over that He would provide the Lamb. In the book of Exodus, the Jews were told to take a perfect lamb that God provided and place the lamb's blood over their doors. When God saw the blood, He wouldn't bring any harm to anyone inside the house. Later, the prophet Isaiah said that a Messiah was coming who would be like a lamb (Isaiah 53:7).

In the gospel of John, Jesus comes to John the Baptist to be baptized. And when John sees Jesus, he says, "Behold, the Lamb of God, who takes away the sin of the world" (John 1:29).

Do you see it? People throughout history had been praying and crying out to God to send a lamb. Send a messiah. Send a substitute just as the lamb was substituted for Isaac. And God sent Jesus. Jesus is the Lamb of God. God has provided the Lamb. Glory to God!

One day in heaven all followers of Jesus will attend a wedding feast called the marriage supper of the Lamb. To be a part of this incredible feast, you need a perfect substitute to shed blood and take your place upon the cross. And that is just what Jesus, the Lamb of God, did! He takes away the sin of the whole world.

> **The next day he [John the Baptist] saw Jesus coming toward him, and said, "Behold, the Lamb of God, who takes away the sin of the world!"**
> **—John 1:29**

Dear Jesus, the Lamb of God,

Thank You for being the perfect substitute for me. Thank You for being the one the world had been waiting for.

I'm grateful for the plan of God to provide a lamb as a substitute for me. Because You were willing to be that sacrificial lamb, I can now live. Thank You that one day, all who love Jesus will attend a wedding feast in heaven, the marriage supper of the Lamb. Until that day, help me to love and follow the Lamb of God every day of my life.

I pray in the name of my Jesus, the Lamb of God.
Amen

Jesus is called...

The Lamb of God—John 1:29

The Names in John's Revelation

When you are asleep, do you dream? Maybe you have happy dreams where you are with all your friends. Maybe you've had a dream where you eat as much ice cream as you want! Do you remember the details of your dreams when you wake up? Sometimes it can be really hard to remember what you dreamed about.

One of the very best friends of Jesus was the apostle John. He wrote the gospel of John, three important letters, and a book God gave to him

in a dream. One night, the Lord caused John to have an amazing dream that we call a vision. God allowed John to dream about events that will one day happen. And the Lord helped John remember everything he dreamed. John wrote it all down in a book we call the Revelation of John. In this amazing look into the future, John gives us some incredible names of Jesus.

John uses many of the same names for Jesus that he used when writing his gospel: the Christ, the Son of Man, the Son of God, and the Lamb. In Revelation, John also introduces many new names.

John writes that Jesus is the Alpha and the Omega. That means that Jesus is A to Z. He is from beginning to end. Jesus is everything, from start to finish. He holds everything together. Nothing is outside of His control.

John says Jesus is the Lion of the Tribe of Judah too! Genesis tells a story about Judah, one of the sons of Jacob. Judah had a dark, messy heart. Because of his sinful heart, he did some awful things to other people. But God changed Judah's heart. Judah's life was changed so much that he offered to give up his life for one of his brothers. Jesus, who lived a perfect life, *did* sacrifice His life. He died on a cross for all His children. Judah is a wonderful reminder that anyone can be changed by Jesus.

John also calls Jesus the Bright Morning Star! In the middle of darkness and sadness, the Bright Morning Star can always be seen. It is faithfully in the same place day after day, year after year. Jesus is our constant, never-changing, never-ending Friend. Bright stars guide people, just as the Bethlehem star guided the wise men to Jesus when they came to worship Him. Jesus will guide you too.

John also says there is a name of Jesus that no one knows except God the Father. It's kind of like a special, secret name. Why would God keep a name of Jesus a secret? Because the Unknown Name of Jesus is too awesome and amazing for any mind to understand. It is too remarkable to take in, too breathtaking to understand, and too astounding to explain. One day when you stand in front of God in heaven, you will learn the unknown name of Jesus. What a glorious day that will be!

Jesus has so many magnificent names because there are so many wonderful things about Him! We have so much to learn and so much to love about Jesus, our Savior and Friend. Thank You, Jesus!

Dear Jesus, the Beginning and the End,

You are the First and the Last. All things in this universe are held together by Your powerful hand.

One day I hope to be with You in heaven and call You by Your amazing unknown name.

Until then, even on the darkest and saddest days, You are the Bright Morning Star. You give light and hope to everyone. Thank You for guiding me, every day of my life.

I pray in the name of Jesus, the Lion of the Tribe of Judah. Amen.

> And one of the elders said to me, "Weep no more; behold, the Lion of the tribe of Judah, the Root of David, has conquered, so that he can open the scroll and its seven seals." And between the throne and the four living creatures and among the elders I saw a Lamb standing, as though it had been slain, with seven horns and with seven eyes, which are the seven spirits of God sent out into all the earth. —Revelation 5:5–6

Some of the new names Jesus is called in Revelation...

Faithful Witness, Firstborn of the Dead, Ruler of the Kings of the Earth—Revelation 1:5

Alpha and Omega—Revelation 1:8   **First and Last**—Revelation 1:17

The One Who Holds the Seven Stars—Revelation 2:1

The One Who Has the Key of David—Revelation 3:7

The Amen—Revelation 3:14   **The Root of David**—Revelation 5:5

The Lamb Who Has Been Slain—Revelation 5:6

Rider on a White Horse—Revelation 19:11–16

The Bright Morning Star—Revelation 22:16

Jesus Knows Your Name

Have you ever adopted a new pet? Maybe it was a puppy or a tiny kitty. Did you get to help choose the pet's name? I'm guessing you thought of a lot of great ideas before finally choosing a name you loved for your new friend.

Your own name was likely chosen with a lot of thought too. Before you were born, your parents probably talked about many different possibilities for what they would call you. Maybe they picked out a list of names to think about and then decided on the perfect one. You may have been named after your mom or dad. Perhaps you were given the name of a grandparent or special family member. No matter what your parents named you, your name is special because it's yours!

Did you know that names have meanings? Maybe your parents chose your name because of its meaning. Your name might mean "strong," "happy," "courageous," or "gentle."

Maybe you have a neighbor named *Mark*. His name means "warrior." Perhaps your best friend is named *Megan*. Her name means "pearl." The name *Sarah* means "princess." The name *Paige* means "helper," and the name *Rachel* means "purity." Those are just a few examples of the meanings of names. One day, if you have children of your own, you might choose a name with a very special meaning.

Don't you love when someone tells you that you have a nice name? Maybe they tell you that your name sounds strong. Or your name is so pretty. Think also about how you feel when someone makes fun of your name. It hurts because your name is special. It is a part of you. It was chosen for you by people who love you.

Did you know that Jesus knows your name? Think about that. The next time you are outside on a pitch-dark night, look up into the sky and see how many stars you can count. The same magnificent Artist who created every single star knows your name. He knows everything about you! He knows exactly how many hairs you have on your head. He knew about you before creation. There is not one single moment of one single day that He stops thinking about you. He knows you fully, and He loves you fully.

Jesus not only knows your name; He loves your name. He loves you.

Throughout this book, we have learned about so many of the magnificent names of Jesus. Are you surprised that Jesus had so many names? Did you know they all tell us beautiful things about Him?

Each of these names helps us to know how to pray to Jesus. When you are afraid of the dark, you can pray to Jesus the Light. When you are feeling lost, you can pray to the Good Shepherd. When you are feeling discouraged, you can pray to the Hope of the World. And when you feel alone, you can pray to Jesus, your brother and your friend.

As you grow, we pray you become more like Jesus as you love and serve Him.

We hope that one day as you come into a room or reach out to those who are hurting, people will say your name and think of Jesus, the One you serve.

Dear Jesus,

Thank You for knowing and loving my name. And thank You for loving me.

Every day, please help me to remember that You are always with me and that You are more important than the food I eat, the water I drink, the sleep I need, and the air I breathe.

I'm thankful for each of Your wonderful names. Throughout my life, help me to call out to You, using Your powerful and wonderful names. Help me to never forget that You are the Door, the Bread, the Master, and the Christ. You are the Son of Man and the Son of God. You are the Carpenter, the Bridegroom, and the Physician. You are the Lord Jesus Christ, my God and my Savior.

I pray in the magnificent name of Jesus, my Lord and God and Savior. Amen.

> "Why, even the hairs of your head are all numbered. Fear not; you are of more value than many sparrows."
> —Luke 12:7

Here are just some of the names Jesus calls you...

Chosen—John 15:18–19   **His beloved**—John 15:9

Child of God—Matthew 5:9, John 1:12   **His friend**—John 15:15

One who has everlasting life—John 3:16   **His servant**—Luke 16:13

A believer—John 14:1   **A child of the King**—Matthew 5:9

His brother—John 20:17   **Salt and light of the earth**—Matthew 5:13–16

Disciple—Matthew 28:19–20   **Fishers of men**—Matthew 4:19

The Magnificent

King
Friend
Living Water
Sir (the One to Whom Respect Is Due)
The Light
The Son of Mary and Joseph
Carpenter
Good Shepherd
Jesus of Nazareth
Prophet
Great Physician
Savior of the World
True Vine
Lamb of God
The Door
Stairway to Heaven

Names of Jesus

Man Lord Holy One Christ God

Great I AM Son of Man

Teacher

Hope of Israel One Who Came Down from Heaven

God's Chosen Master Horn of Salvation

Big Brother Bread of Life

The Truth Bridegroom God's Son

Cornerstone The One

Acknowledgments

All honor and praise to the Lord Jesus, our Shepherd, Savior, Redeemer, and King. We pray this book brings glory to Your name. You alone are worthy.

An enormous thank you to Michelle Freeman and her team at B&H Publishing Group and Lifeway Christian Resources. This book would not have happened apart from your passion to help children learn to pray the names of Jesus. It has been a delight to work alongside you, Michelle. Thank you for caring deeply about this book and guiding it from a rough idea to a beautiful reality.

Thank you to Andrew Wolgemuth for championing this book. Your wisdom, expertise, and constant encouragement were an essential part of this project. We are grateful for our lengthy friendship.

Thank you to Paran Kim, our extraordinary illustrator. It has been an honor to work with you. We knew you were the perfect artist the first time we saw your beautiful illustrations. You have an incredible gift. Thank you for using it for God's glory.

A heartfelt thank you to Gary Ascanio, our most faithful prayer partner, who has covered this book in prayer since day one.

Thank you to our parents, Roger and Madelyn Franzke and Herb and Alice Dodd. You instilled in us a joy for reading, a love for children, and an appreciation for art that long ago laid the foundation for this book. This book is in many ways a tribute to you.

Thanks to our friends who have helped us to see Jesus more clearly. Thank you to Cindy Limbrick, Elizabeth George, Matt Appling, Becky Mercer, Lynne Dykstra, Jill Kapple, Katie Metcalf, Liz Nelson, Amy Royston, and Kris and Adrienne McGee. We treasure your friendship and how you spur us on to love the Lord.

A Note from Sally

In the spring of 2020, COVID-19 shocked all of us as we suddenly faced a new way of doing life.

We found ourselves scrambling to figure out how to virtually continue our jobs, church, school, and more. As a teacher, I was desperately trying to teach my young class of kindergarteners over video from our home while partnering with parents to make sure the children felt connected and secure.

It has been a time of uncertainty, but many of us can point also to the rich blessings we may have not experienced otherwise—bonus time with family, new ways to participate in worship, and times of seeing God's gracious care through life's joys and deep sorrows. For me and Jimmy, lockdown provided a special opportunity to discuss the reality of this book and the margin to write.

Years ago, Jimmy had done the initial research into the names of Jesus in the Gospels. He created chapter outlines with a particular area of emphasis. Now it was my job to write each chapter before returning to Jimmy for the initial editing.

During lockdown, I would teach my Kinders from my home each morning. Then in the early afternoon, I would make my way into my empty classroom to write. The quiet was at times unnerving as the room should have been filled with activity and noise. I pulled up my Circle Chair and faced the empty space that would normally be filled with my little ones ready to listen. I pictured each little face. I thought through how I would speak to them about each magnificent name of Jesus.

I anticipated little hands being raised to ask questions. I imagined hearing, "What does that mean?" from those who loved clarification, always keeping me on my toes. I pictured the insights that would come from young hearts processing the power of God's Word. I visualized their sweet faces as they wrapped their young minds around the majesty of Jesus.

The writing of this book brought much healing to my heart as I grieved not being with my students. I found it brought closure to a school year when normally each child is prayed over individually and sent out to continue his or her journey toward a love for learning. So, although this book was written in an empty kindergarten classroom, it was inspired by Evie, Jaclyn, Noah, Cecil, Olive, Naomi, Kingsley, Elliana, Reese, Wesley, Jeremiah, Shiloh, and Mariana as well as Calder, Timothy, Elizabeth, Norah, Eleanor, Zef, Rome, Ford, Lucy, Clark, Ada, Adella, and Isaac. Thank you, kids, for encouraging your teacher to write this book. May you not only grow in your love of learning but also, more importantly, in your love for our Lord Jesus.

Remember, Mrs. Dodd loves you!

How to Pray with Your Child

One of our children once asked Jimmy, "What is the best prayer I can pray?" After thinking through the great prayers in the Bible, Jimmy responded, "I think the best prayer is, 'Dear Jesus, help me.'"

That seems too easy, right?

Prayer can feel intimidating. We may be bewildered as we wonder how to begin or what to say. We may feel at a loss, fearing that our words won't be adequate for God. The idea of teaching our children to pray, when we are not sure how to do it ourselves, seems quite daunting.

When we pray to God, it is essential that we remember several things. First and foremost, God loves us. Second, God is not mad at us.

He knows that we are all broken and that there is no one who does not desperately need Him. And third, just as you would not turn away a good friend who wanted to talk to you, God does not turn His back or make light of what we have to say. God loves to hear people lift their voices and turn their hearts to Him.

Prayer is having a conversation with God as if He were sitting right with you. God is the creator of the world, and He already knows everything about us. We can't surprise God.

Begin teaching your child to pray by modeling praying out loud to God. As your child hears you talk to God, they commonly imitate the very things you pray. The prayers at the end of each chapter in this book are a wonderful place to start. Consider praying the prayer one sentence at a time and asking your child to repeat your words. As this becomes a regular habit, children will often begin to talk to God in their own unique way. It is precious to hear them as they talk to the Father.

Our own children have prayed in their own way. One of our daughters wanted to pray for Disney princesses, nightly going through a list of every princess she could remember (which was all of them). We encouraged her to also pray for "real people," not wanting to squelch what she felt was important but gently directing her to the needs of others in our *real* day-to-day life.

Praying out loud takes practice, but we can be confident knowing that our words are precious and being heard by the only One who loves us immensely and unconditionally.

About the Authors

Jimmy Dodd is an author, well-known speaker, and the founder and CEO of PastorServe. Working across denominational lines, PastorServe exists to strengthen the Church by serving pastors. Jimmy serves a number of ministries including Cross International and Unite KC. Jimmy is husband to Sally and father to five amazing kids.

Sally Dodd has been married to Jimmy for 38 years. She loves being a wife, mom and grandmother, and a kindergarten teacher. As a child, Sally wanted to be a teacher or a pink ballerina. The ballerina thing didn't quite work out, so she is thankful to be able to invest in the lives of children.

About the Illustrator

Paran Kim grew up in Seoul, South Korea, and moved to Tokyo when she was 20 to study fine art. She has traveled a lot and had various jobs including being an art teacher for children and a career at a nursing home. However, she realized her true passion lay in making picture books and became a full-time illustrator. Paran now lives in Dresden, Germany, with her husband. When she is not drawing, she loves singing and playing the guitar.

Jesus, the Beginning and the End